Managing Business Intelligence Projects

Dr. Macedonio Alanís

Tecnologico de Monterrey

Imprint

Any Brand names and product names mentioned in this book are subject to trademark, Brand or patent protection and are trademarks or registered trademarks of their respective holders. The use of brand names, product names, common names, trade names, product descriptions, etc. even without a particular marking in this work is in no way to be construed to mean that such names may be regarded as unrestricted in respect of trademark and brand protection legislation and could thus be used by anyone.

Cover image photo by Path Digital on Unsplash

ISBN-13: 9798878662345

ASIN e-book: B0CV3B73W7

ASIN printed version: B0CV4CKSJR

https://www.amazon.com/-/e/B08529L1PZ

https://www.amazon.com/author/alanis

alanis@tec.mx   maalanis@hotmail.com

Dedication

For Jacobo, Pablo, and Cristóbal

Acknowledgements

This book is the product of multiple meetings to prepare curriculum recommendations for information technology, computer science, digital transformation, and business intelligence programs at Tecnologico de Monterrey. Many professors and specialists from different campuses of Tecnologico de Monterrey collaborated with ideas and content that have made this work possible. To all of them, my infinite thanks and appreciation.

I would like to thank Alberto López Hernández, Itzel Alejandra Zarate Solís, and Bernardo Charles Canales for their support in reviewing the topics to be included in the book—special thanks to Pablo Raúl García Velazco for his work on the content of chapter three. I would also like to thank Eduardo Esteva Armida, Celia Fabiola Vásquez García, and Gabriel Héctor Carmona Olmos for participating in the initial content discussions.

Table of Contents

Extended Table of Contents

Module I

Identifying Business Intelligence Solutions

Chapter 1

A Framework for Business Intelligence Systems

"On two occasions I have been asked, —"Pray, Mr. Babbage, if you put into the machine wrong figures, will the right answers come out?" In one case a member of the Upper, and in the other a member of the Lower, House put this question. I am not able rightly to apprehend the kind of confusion of ideas that could provoke such a question."

Charles Babbage, "Passages from the life of a philosopher", 1864.

1.1.- Learning objectives

- Define business intelligence systems.
- Compare and contrast business intelligence systems and information systems.
- Identify the components of a business intelligence system.
- Understand the difference between data and information.
- Identify the attributes of useful information.
- Understanding the concept of information overload.

1.2.- The Complexity of Creating Business Intelligence Solutions

Technology can support decision-making by providing complete and timely information or enabling more complex data analysis. The ultimate goal of these projects is to help the organization fulfill its mission: to increase sales, reduce operating costs, or improve market positioning.

However, a computer alone is not good for much. Computers need programs or software, data, and they need to be used correctly to have any positive effect on the company. Understanding technology's potential requires viewing it not only as a piece of computer equipment but also as a comprehensive solution, as a system where all its parts contribute to achieving the company's objectives. A company that leverages technology to improve its processes and make better decisions needs to understand how to select the problems to attack, how to build or acquire the necessary equipment and software, how to obtain the required information, and how to operate these solutions.

This book presents the processes for selecting, creating, and implementing business intelligence solutions. The discussion is divided into five modules:

1. Identifying Business Intelligence Solutions
2. Valuation and prioritization of business intelligence projects
3. Development of business intelligence solutions
4. The Information Technology Industry
5. Next Steps for Business Intelligence

The discussion begins with the identification of the elements of a business intelligence solution, and an analysis of their contribution to the decision-making process.

1.3.- What is a business intelligence system?

The broadest definition of business intelligence is "An umbrella term that combines the architectures, tools, databases, analytical tools, applications, and methodologies to support the decision-making process." [Sharda, Delen & Turban, 2015]

This definition is consistent with the more general definition of an information system, which is:

"An integrated user-machine system to provide information that supports operations, management, and decision-making functions in an organization. The system uses computer equipment and software; manual procedures; models for analysis, planning, control, and decision-making; and a database." [Davis & Olson, 1985]

Combining both definitions, we find that:

A business intelligence system is:

- An integrated user-machine system
- For providing information
- To support the decision-making process
- In an organization

The system uses:

- Computer Architectures and Equipment
- Analytical Tools & Applications
- Databases
- Manual Procedures
- And methodologies to support the decision-making process.

The central component in this definition is the user (who makes the decision). The system also needs a computer (hardware) and programs (software) to operate. But the system is not just the computer and software. It also requires manual procedures before, during, and after processing and data on which the analyses will be carried out. Figure 1.1 illustrates the components of a business intelligence system.

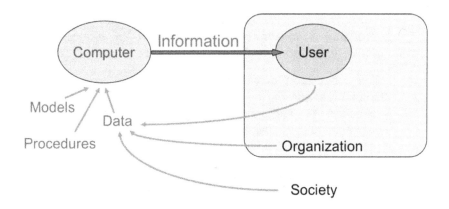

Figure 1.1 – Components of a business intelligence system

In a system, it is possible to identify four essential activities:

- **Input**, which feeds data into the system.
- **Process**, converts the received data into useful information at different stages.
- **Output**, which delivers the processed information to the user.
- The fourth activity, called **feedback**, uses a system's output as input for future adjustments and processing.

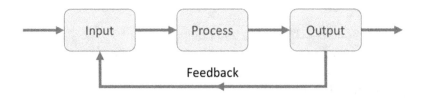

Figure 1.2 – Essential activities in a system

In the case of the package delivery company described in the Minicase below, the capture of the parcel tracking number made by the employee at reception represents an input. The system then generates outputs indicating the route to be followed by the package or truck where it is to be loaded. These outputs are converted back into feedback as they can be used (compared with input from the package position receiver in-route) to validate the packet's position at a given time and to calculate the next stage of the route. Finally, when the package is delivered, the receipt signature is captured in the system (input) and saved in a database that stores the

> **Minicase - Information management in a package delivery company**
>
> The process is only partially computerized in a parcel company's tracking system. It all starts when a customer takes the package to the receiving office. Upon receiving the package, an employee assigns it a label with a tracking number and enters the data into the system. Different mechanisms and people record the package's passage through different stations during transport. When the package arrives at its destination, the truck driver delivers it to the recipient, records the delivery time, and collects the recipient's signature, which closes the process.

information. The system can then issue a report (output) to the sender of the package advising them that the package has been delivered.

This definition shows that business intelligence is not a single component. From a functional point of view, there are three subsystems: the data subsystem, the analysis subsystem, and the user. The first element gathers and prepares data from different sources. The second one processes the data into useful information that is received by the third component, the user, who is the one who takes advantage of the results to generate value for the organization.

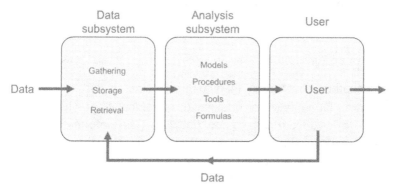

Figure 1.3 – Functional components of a business intelligence system

1.4.- Characteristics of the information

Data items can represent something about the world (the package weighs 450 grams, it was received at 11:45 a.m., the destination was in Mexico City, the price charged was $350, etc.). The data itself says little. When data is organized in a certain way, it can have valuable meaning for certain people. For example, the transportation cost can be calculated based on the package's weight, volume, and route. Compared with the price charged for delivery, this cost can show how profitable it is to deliver packages on that route or if the company should try to change the price for its services.

Therefore, while data represents reality, information is defined as data organized to mean something to someone (remember that people receive the information to make the decisions). Data is the input; information is the output.

Information aims to reduce uncertainty and supports the decision-making process. Inaccurate information that arrives after the decision has been made or that is misunderstood is not very useful or can even lead us to make bad decisions. Therefore, the information must be of high quality. Senn [1987] identifies a series of "information attributes" that define quality information:

Attributes of an Information Set

- Relevant: It is necessary for a particular situation.
- Comprehensive: Provides the user with everything they need about a specific problem.
- Timely: Is available when needed.

Attributes of an information item

- Accuracy: Represents the situation or state as it is.
- Form: Quantitative or qualitative, numerical or graphic, printed or electronic, summarized or detailed. The information's format selection is dictated by the situation in which it will be used.
- Frequency: A measure of how often it is required or produced.
- Extension: It can cover a wide area of interest or just a part of it.
- Origin: Internal or external, direct or indirect
- Temporality: Information can be oriented to the past, present, or future activities or events.

1.5.- The value of information

Sometimes, the effect of having the information needed to make a decision can be quantifiable. For example, when deciding whether to invest some money in a fixed or variable rate instrument. Suppose the information indicates that the variable return will remain 1% above the fixed rate offered on the first instrument. In that case, having that information in time produces a return of that 1% on the investment.

Other times, the decision is probabilistic, which means one can make the best decision. Still, the situation can move in different directions, so one makes the best decision with available information. Better information could mean improving the likelihood of better results (although that couldn't be assured entirely). Investing in a company's stock depends on whether our information points to those shares rising in price. However, many variables determine the stock price at a given time, some outside the company's

8

control, so the investment decision is based on the best available information. Still, there is no absolute certainty of the final result.

Another example of the value of information in probabilistic decisions could be seen in horse racing. If seven horses are running, and we don't have data on them, the probability of picking the winning horse in a bet at the start of the race would be one-seventh. Now, if someone tells me that the number one horse is sick and has no chance of winning, I can safely rule out the possibility of that horse winning, so now the chance of picking the winning horse is one in six (better than before).

Minicase – Information in Mexico's Voter Cards

Every citizen of Mexico over 18 receives a voter's card. The card includes the name, address, photograph, fingerprint, and signature of its owner. With this information, the card's bearer can be identified on election day, and officers at voting centers can decide whether to give the individual a ballot. The cards do not include the subject's weight since obtaining this information would be expensive (putting scales in each center, training the operators, collecting the data, etc.). It would not add more certainty to the identification. If the photograph, fingerprints, and signature recorded on a card cannot tell if the bearer is its legitimate owner, having information on the subject's weight would not make the identification decision more accurate. Deciding what information to include in a report is one of the most critical responsibilities of a business process designer.

1.6.- Information overload

If we map the amount (quantity) of information received against the quality of the decision made, it can be argued that more information produces better decisions; however, there are two factors to consider. First, sometimes new information only confirms the previous one, so it does not provide added value, and the second is that it is humans who make the decision, so the information must be understandable and actionable by a person.

There comes a point where too much information can confuse the decision-maker, and their performance can get worse. This point is known as the point of information overload.

The point of information overload is where providing more information to a decision-maker results in lower-quality decisions (due to confusion or failure in human processing of the data). Figure 1.3 illustrates the relationship between information quality and decision quality and identifies the point of information overload.

Another essential aspect to consider is the cost/benefit ratio of the information. The cost (in time, resources, and money) required to obtain the data must be weighed against the expected benefit of having it. Sometimes, the price is so high that the information loses its potential value.

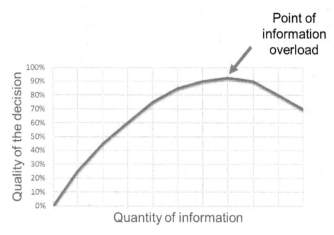

Figure 1.4 – Point of information overload

1.7.- Summary

- In its broadest definition, a business intelligence system is "An umbrella term that combines the architectures, tools, databases, analytical tools, applications, and methodologies to support the decision-making process."
- A business intelligence system is defined as an integrated user-machine system for providing information that supports the decision-making process in an organization. The system uses

Computer architectures and equipment, analytical tools and applications, databases, manual procedures, and methodologies to support decision-making.

- The building blocks of a system are inputs, processes, outputs, and feedback.
- From a functional point of view, there are three subsystems in a business intelligence solution: the data subsystem, the analysis subsystem, and the user. The first element gathers and prepares data from different sources. The second one processes the data into useful information that is received by the third component, the user, who is the one who takes advantage of the results to generate value for the organization.
- For information to be valuable, it must be relevant, complete, and timely. Individual pieces of information must be accurate and come in the correct format, as often as required, with the right length, source, and timing.
- The quantity of information is not proportional to the quality of the decision. More information might not increase the value of a decision, and there is a point of information overload where more information decreases the quality of the output or where the cost of producing information exceeds the value it represents for the decision.

1.8.- Review exercises

Questions

1. What is a business intelligence system?
2. What is an information system?
3. Why do we say that a business intelligence system is so much more than just a computer?
4. What is the difference between data and information?
5. What is the difference between hardware and software?
6. What does information overload mean?
7. What are the essential characteristics of the information?
8. What happens if the information received for a decision arrives late?
9. What happens if the information received for a decision needs to be corrected?

Exercises

1. Identify a process in a real organization and describe its inputs, processes, outputs, and feedback.
2. Identify a restaurant's inputs, processes, and outputs when receiving a pizza order over the phone.
3. What are the inputs, processes, and outputs of the process that a doctor follows when diagnosing a disease in a patient?
4. Look for an example where too much information makes a decision more complicated.
5. Find a case where the cost of obtaining some information is higher than the value it might bring to a decision.

Chapter 2

Technology in Decision Making

"This is only a foretaste of what is to come, and only the shadow of what is going to be. We have to have some experience with the machine before we really know its capabilities. It may take years before we settle down to the new possibilities, but I do not see why it should not enter any one of the fields normally covered by the human intellect, and eventually compete on equal terms."

Alan Turing, "The Mechanical Brain. Answer Found to 300-Year-Old Problem", The Times, 1949.

2.1.- Learning objectives

- Recognize the different types of decisions.
- Identify the different kinds of information systems.
- Recognize the objectives of different information systems.
- Understand the functions of different information systems.

2.2.- Levels of management in an organization

Decision-making requires information. The information comes from both external sources and sources internal to the organization. A company has no single information system to get all the data. In reality, the data comes from several different systems. Computers can help in the company's operation, inventory management, sales, administrative control, and even in the business's accounting. Often, this is achieved using independent systems, and all of them are possible data sources for business intelligence.

To understand data, you need to know how it's generated. An organization has different positions with different needs, depending on whether the focus is on administrative control, strategic planning, or operational control.

Typically, people use a triangle to represent the levels of management in a company. This type of diagram is known as Anthony's triangle, after Professor Robert Anthony, who came up with the model. In his book "Planning and Control Systems: A Framework for Analysis" [Anthony, 1965], he identifies three organizational levels, as illustrated in Figure 2.1.

The operational level is where the products are manufactured, the customer is served, and the boxes are packed and delivered. The focus is "ensuring that specific activities are carried out effectively and efficiently."

The tactical level, which Anthony calls the administrative level, focuses on "ensuring that resources are obtained and used effectively and efficiently to achieve the organization's objectives."

The strategic level is where "the organization's goals, changes to those goals, the resources to be used to achieve the goals, and the policies that govern the acquisition, use, and disposition of those resources are decided."

At the strategic level, the organization's future is planned. At the tactical level, strategic plans are landed, and operational problems are resolved. At the operational level, work is being done to solve the issues of the present. If an operator is solving the problems of the present, they don't have time to think about tomorrow; that is the leader's job, to focus on the future.

Figure 2.1 – Levels in an organization

2.3.- Types of decisions

The role of computers is also different at different organizational levels. More than fifty years ago, Robert Anthony wrote: "At the level of administrative control, the judgment and feelings of human beings dominate; In computers, that's necessarily absent. In strategic planning, a company-wide model can be a valuable tool for examining the organizational implications of a proposed strategy. At the operational control level, models for area-specific control are essential, and computer use is common." [Anthony, 1965]

One of the reasons for the different roles of technology is that there are different types of work and decisions at each level. Two main types of decisions are identified: structured decisions and unstructured decisions [Gorry & Scott-Morton, 1971].

Structured decisions are those that have a defined procedure. It may not be simple, but there are several steps to follow to make the decision. For example, a teller's decision to pay a check at a bank counter may be complex, but it has strict rules. The rules are clear:

- The account must exist.
- The signatures on the check and the account must match.
- The available balance in the account must be greater than the amount of the check (among other things).

15

Another example of a structured decision is the reorder point in a retail store. If we know that the supplier takes two days to restock an item and that item sells two units per day, we would have to order a new shipment when there are at least four units left in stock, thus avoiding leaving the store without inventory. That decision has rules: The company must issue a refill order when the inventory goes down to four units.

Unstructured decisions are those where the decision-maker must bring criteria, evaluation, and understanding to the definition of the problem. For example, deciding where to build a new supermarket in a particular location requires information about expected traffic and ground conditions. However, it also requires understanding the typical customer in that area and an idea of what would be expected for that part of the city. Other unstructured decisions would be in the area of human resources. When you decide to hire someone, it's not just because of their credentials; a recruiter interviews the candidate, and based on what happens in the interview, an experienced specialist can tell whether or not the candidate is suitable for the position. The response to an unstructured decision is "felt," though we can't say precisely what it should feel like.

It is possible to identify decisions of all kinds at all levels. However, at the operational level, most decisions tend to be structured, while at the strategic level, decisions tend to be unstructured, as shown in Figure 2.2

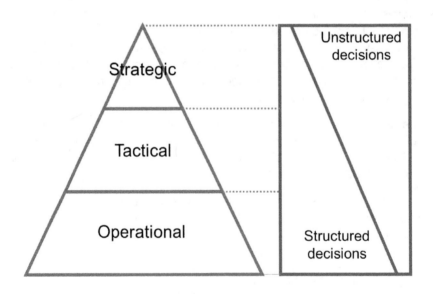

Figure 2.2 – Types of decisions at every organizational level

2.4.- Types of information systems

Transaction Processing Systems

Most organizations' operations are based on some well-understood structured transactions (sales, accounting, purchasing, etc.). Most structured transactions can be programmed into a computer system. These systems are known as transaction processing systems (TPS). They record and process the daily transactions needed to operate a business. They generally exist at the operational level.

Examples of transaction processing systems would be systems for processing payroll, accounts receivable, accounts payable, inventories, etc.

In a supermarket, sales, inventory, and personnel management systems are examples of transaction processing systems. Their reports serve to answer operational questions that occur daily in the business.

Management Information Systems

Management information systems, or information reporting systems (MIS or IRS), support the tactical level of the organization. Generally, they use data from the company's internal transactions and present it in condensed form or by identifying points out of range to facilitate managerial decisions. Almost always, for their data, they use the outputs of transaction processing systems.

In the case of the supermarket, the store manager doesn't need to know precisely how many cans of tuna or bars of soap are in the store. The manager needs to know whether the inventory level of any essential products is dangerously low or if they have too many units of some perishable product. That would help the manager target the store's advertising campaigns or the distribution of products on the sales floor. Systems for sales analysis, marketing campaign guidance, or production planning represent these systems.

Decision support systems

The job of an information system is to support the decision-making process. However, unstructured decisions have no known process. How can a computer be programmed to provide the necessary support in those cases?

The answer is that, even if we don't know how a decision is made, we know that a human being makes this decision and needs to see the available information to analyze it and get a sense of the present situation. Based on the available information, the user makes the best possible decision at their discretion.

Decision support systems use internal and external information and require tools to visualize and manipulate the data. A user "plays" with the data until it "says" something and decides.

So, a decision support system (DSS) helps managers make unique, constantly changing decisions that can't be specified in advance.

In the case of the supermarket, decisions such as the location of a new store, investment planning, or the launch of global marketing campaigns could be supported with decision support systems.

Figure 2.3 illustrates the relationship between organizational levels and types of information systems.

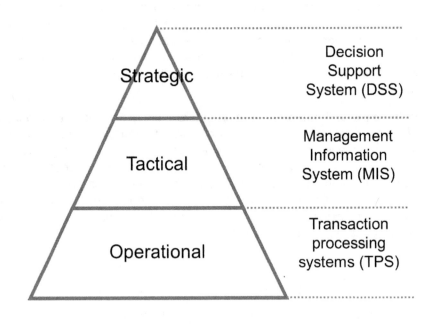

Figure 2.3 – Type of system most likely to prevail at each organizational level

2.5.- Working with data from across the organization

Imagine if an administrator, to make a decision, had to consult several, perhaps hundreds, of information systems installed in the company. None of these systems can communicate with each other, and each one presents different reports. The time it would take to make the decision would be longer than the time available, and the amount of information would surely exceed the point of information overload.

When computers first arrived in companies, independent systems were developed, each built by a different team and with its data. The problem was that when trying to get the systems to communicate and exchange information, it became apparent that each system had a different view of the company. While sales systems focus on customers, engineering systems analyze part or product numbers and accounts systems concentrate on cash flow. When trying to integrate them, the companies realized that this would be an almost impossible job because when one system could connect to its neighbor, the second one had already changed and required a different interface.

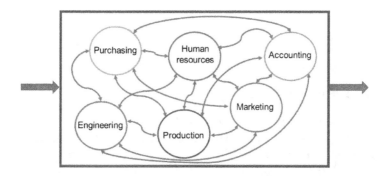

Figure 2.4 – Independent interconnected systems

One solution is the implementation **of enterprise applications**, which are systems that span several functional areas, focus on running business processes across the enterprise, and include all levels of management [Laudon & Laudon, 2019].

There are four main types of business applications:

- Enterprise resource planning systems (ERPs),
- Supply chain management systems (SCM),
- Customer relationship management systems (CRMs)
- Knowledge management systems (KMS)

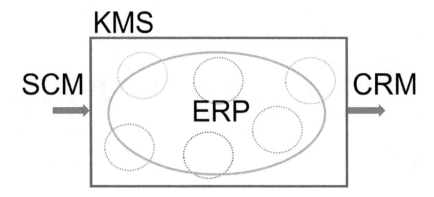

Figure 2.5 – Integrated enterprise applications

Enterprise Resource Planning Systems (ERP)

Enterprise resource planning systems (ERP) integrate manufacturing and production, sales and marketing, accounting and finance, and human resources into a single, coordinated system. An ERP provides a single system for the company's vital internal processes. This way, when production needs an employee to work overtime, the payroll and accounting are automatically updated. When a sale is completed, production and purchases are automatically updated.

An ERP automates many business processes associated with operational or production aspects. The system gathers data from all processes and stores it in a central database that all components share.

ERP systems are modular; a company can acquire one or more modules and integrate different functionality into its system.

They are configurable, meaning they can be adjusted to meet the needs of a business. For example, one company may allow a buyer to authorize transactions of up to $10,000 and require the department director's signature for purchases exceeding that sum, while for another, the limit might be $150,000 or require two signatures. Typically, the configuration is done by an external company that analyzes the processes and enters the business rules into the system.

The advantages of ERP systems are having a complete view of the company, coordinating different functions, and a relatively quick implementation of the system. An ERP solution can cost anywhere from two thousand to more than ten million dollars, depending on the company's size and the operation's difficulty. It can take a couple of months to two years to complete. However, the cost savings and efficiencies that come with an ERP more than justify the investment.

A disadvantage of ERPs is that if the company has no defined processes, it would be difficult to implement a system that automates processes that do not exist. In addition, complex training is required for users and staff who maintain and develop modules of the company's ERP.

Examples of ERP system vendors available in the market are SAP, Oracle, and Microsoft. Some companies that provide consulting services for implementing ERP solutions are Accenture, Deloitte, IBM, Capgemini, EY, and PwC. [Faith, et al., 2020; DiCapua et al., 2020].

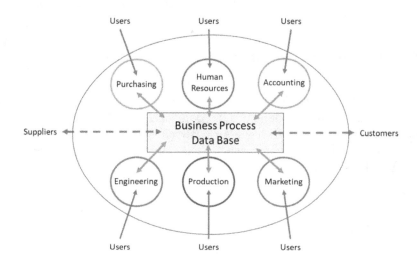

Figure 2.6 – Model of an ERP system

21

Supply Chain Management Systems (SCM)

The most efficient production line with the best sales force is only valuable if the company can procure the raw materials required for the products. Regardless of how many bicycles a company sells, there will only be production if they purchase and receive the necessary tires.

Supply chain management systems (SCM) focus on coordinating purchasing and transportation activities for raw materials and finished products, ensuring supply at the lowest possible cost and reducing inventories to a minimum without affecting production. Companies generally have enough raw material inventory to respond to production demands; however, the money invested in inventory is recovered when the end product is manufactured and sold, so having a high inventory level leads to high financial costs.

In theory, the ideal inventory level is zero; this practice is known as Just In Time. It requires such coordination that the parts arrive from the manufacturer when production requires them for the final product assembly. It is as if when the parts are taken off the truck from the supplier, they are installed directly into the end products. Doing this requires excellent coordination between the participants in the production chain. It is very complex because a mistake by any of the participants would jeopardize the stability of the entire group. A certain inventory level is always needed, although intended to be as low as possible without jeopardizing production.

Some leading supply chain management solutions providers are Oracle, SAP, Blue Yonder, Kinaxis, E2open, and Logility. [Salley, et al., 2021]

Customer Relationship Management Systems (CRM)

Customer relationship management (CRM) systems focus on managing customer interactions. They use information from a customer's interaction with the company to identify their potential, retain the customer, and increase sales. A CRM answers questions such as: who are our best customers? What are they buying? And where are they? CRMs support sales in three stages: pre-sales, sales, and post-sales.

Pre-sales systems coordinate the company's marketing efforts, help identify leads, manage the sales pipeline, and manage and measure the effectiveness of advertising campaigns.

Sales process support systems simplify the salesperson's job when facing a customer, offer systems for presenting quotes, package configurators, contact information, and even tools to calculate sales staff commissions (so that they spend their time selling instead of filling out internal forms to collect their commission).

Post-sales systems handle warranties and customer service. The management of the customer service center (or call center), answering customer questions or complaints, and handling service calls in case a product has to be repaired are examples of applications of this type.

The leader in CRM solutions is Salesforce, a company that works in the cloud and provides its services over the Internet to its customers in a subscription model. Other ERP vendors include Adobe, Oracle, Microsoft, Creatio, Pegasystems, and ServiceNow. Among the consulting firms that can support the implementation of CRM solutions are Deloitte, Accenture, IBM, Capgemini, and PwC. [Hansen, et al., 2020; Manusama & LeBlanc, 2020; Sparks, et al., 2020]

Mincase – Sales support systems changed the way people buy cars.

A few years ago, in automotive dealerships, if a customer walked in and asked for the price of a car with specific options such as leather seats, deluxe tires, sound system, etc. The salesperson took note of the request and had to consult several manuals to calculate the car's final price. This process could take up to half a day. The client had to return the next morning to learn how much the requested options would cost.

Today, the process is different:

- The customer sits with the salesperson.
- The customer chooses the alternatives he wants in his car.
- The salesman enters them into the computer.

A quote can be printed immediately, including the final price, a photograph of what the car would look like with those options already integrated, the expected delivery date, and financing alternatives. Once clients enter the auto dealership, they can only be let go with a formal offer.

Knowledge Management Systems (KMS)

The value of a company is greater than the price of its buildings, inventory, and bank accounts. A company is worth the price of its tangible and intangible knowledge assets. Understanding the customer, how to best manufacture your products, and how to develop new solutions are intangible assets that can add significant value to an organization.

A knowledge management system (KMS) brings together the company's knowledge and makes it available to whoever needs it at the right time. The functions of a KMS include:

- Knowledge acquisition: the identification and capture of the information to be shared.
- Storage of knowledge in specialized databases.
- Distribute knowledge to those who require it through portals and search engines.
- The application of knowledge through expert systems or decision support systems.

2.7.- Summary

- Decision-making requires information. The information comes from both external sources and sources internal to the organization. A company has no single information system to get all the data. The data comes from several different systems.
- There are three organizational levels: At the strategic level, the organization's future is planned. At the tactical level, strategic plans are landed, and operational problems are resolved. At the operational level, work is being done to solve the issues of the present.
- The role of computers is also different at different organizational levels.
- There are different types of work and decisions at each level. Structured decisions have a defined procedure, unstructured decisions have no rules, and the decision-maker must bring judgment, evaluation, and understanding to the problem definition. There are more structured decisions at the operational level and unstructured at the strategic level.
- As there are different information needs, there are different types of computer systems: TPS records and processes the daily

transactions needed to operate a business. MIS or IRS supports the tactical level of the organization in decisions, and DSS helps managers make unique, constantly changing decisions that cannot be specified in advance.

- Enterprise applications are systems that span multiple functional areas, focus on running business processes across the enterprise, and include all levels of management. There are four types: ERP provides a single system for all critical internal processes of the company, SCM focuses on coordinating purchasing and transportation of raw materials and products, CRM focuses on managing customer interactions, KMS gathers the knowledge of the company and puts it at the fingertips of whoever needs it at the appropriate time.

2.8.- Review exercises

Questions

1. What functions are performed primarily at the strategic level of the organization?
2. What functions are performed mainly at the tactical level of the organization?
3. What functions are performed primarily at the organizational level of the company?
4. Identify three structured decisions that exist in a fast-food restaurant
5. Name four unstructured decisions you might encounter in a shoe factory
6. What are transaction processing systems used for? What kind of decisions do they support?
7. What is the role of management information systems?
8. What is the function of a decision support system?

Exercises

1. Analyze the organizational structure of a company in your region. Classify positions by defining whether they are strategic, tactical, or operational.
2. Find the names of two companies that sell enterprise resource planning (ERP) systems.

3. Locate the webpage of the company SAP. What types of systems are their primary source of income?
4. Find information about the company Salesforce; what kind of technology does it offer? What is it for?

Chapter 3

Data Analytics in Business

"I have no data yet. It is a capital mistake to theorize before one has data. Insensibly one begins to twist facts to suit theories, instead of theories to suit facts."

Sherlock Holmes in "A Scandal in Bohemia," Sir Arthur Conan Doyle, 1891.

3.1.- Learning objectives

- Recognize the three essential components of a business intelligence system.
- Differentiate between descriptive, predictive, and prescriptive analytics.
- Identify challenges and risks in data collection, analysis, and erroneous data types.
- Understand the different tools for the study of information and their general characteristics.
- Recognize the differences between dashboards and scorecards.
- Identify the characteristics of big data.
- Understand the difference between operational data and experiential data and their relevance.
- Understand the ethical challenges and regulations in data security and confidentiality.

3.2.- Descriptive, predictive, and prescriptive analytics

As presented at the beginning of this book, from a functional point of view, a business intelligence system comprises three main components: the data subsystem, the analytics subsystem, and the user.

The data subsystem collects, cleans, and stores the information for decision-making. The information can come from internal or external sources, is temporarily stored in a data warehouse or data mart, and is available for use by the analysis subsystem.

The analysis subsystem consists of mathematical models, tools, and computer programs that allow data to be manipulated to identify trends, statistics, or ways of presenting information to the decision-maker.

The user is the one who receives the results and, based on the information obtained, the context of the decision, and their own experience, decides whether more information is required, another type of processing is needed, or if a decision can be made.

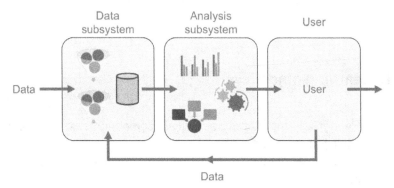

Figure 3.1 – Components of a business intelligence system

Business Intelligence tools can have three main analytical perspectives: descriptive, predictive, and prescriptive. Initially, the tools for each function were differentiated, but it is increasingly common to find applications that integrate functionalities that cover more than one or all three perspectives.

Descriptive Analytics: this allows you to analyze the information that has already happened in an organization, usually to monitor and improve performance. Examples include charts showing inventory turnover, historical year-over-year cost performance trends, market segmentation, measuring customer satisfaction, or results of operations.

Predictive Analytics: allows the analysis of the information recorded, seeking to identify patterns and future trends through regressions. Some examples are forecasts of the days of stock that a commodity is expected to have, an analysis of what items a customer might be interested in taking into account their behavior, potential fraudulent transactions within the behavior of purchases with a credit card, or the financial projection of an organization.

Prescriptive Analytics: allows you to play with scenario simulations, perform sensitivity analysis (also known as "what-if" analysis, where a system yields results depending on imposed assumptions), and optimize results. Examples for this section may include recommendations for inventory replenishment, selecting an investment portfolio to achieve a financial goal, or scenario simulation for determining preventive maintenance in production according to specific symptoms or values.

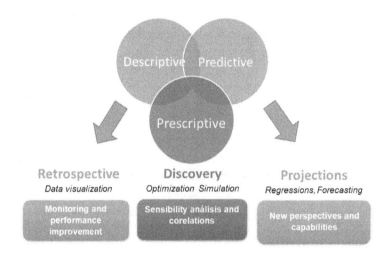

Figure 3.2 - Perspectives of business intelligence

Minicase - Prescription drugs don't sell the way they used to

When a pharmaceutical company develops a new drug, it's essential to make it known to doctors so they can consider it in their prescriptions. To reach doctors, companies have a sales force that usually visits medical professionals in their offices and gives free samples to their patients. The practice has operated almost unchanged for nearly fifty years. However, some in the industry believe that today's doctors prefer to learn about new drugs through electronic means and video conferencing rather than personal visits. What tests are needed to determine if doctors' preferences for new drugs are changing? Can you predict what will happen to a company's sales force in this area? What kind of analysis would explain why those changes occur in the market?

3.3.- The data subsystem

The data subsystem collects, cleans, and stores the information for decision-making. The information can come from sources inside or outside the company. It's usually not convenient to work directly with data from production systems (it wouldn't be fun if someone wanted to analyze a production scenario and cause work on the manufacturing floor to stop). Therefore, the relevant data is copied to a temporary storage called a data warehouse (Data Warehouse or Data Mart). Similarly, relevant external data is extracted and stored in the same container to make it available for analysis. The data subsystem consists of the internal data sources, the external data sources, the data extraction systems, and the data warehouse. A common practice is for the data extraction component to interact with the company's other internal systems and copy the necessary information to the data warehouse. This process usually happens at night, so you have fresh, up-to-date data to work on decisions each day. Suppose part of the data warehouse content is deleted or modified due to an error. In that case, requesting a fresh copy of the information can return to the decision-making process without affecting the organization's regular operation. Similarly, designing extraction systems that constantly update the data warehouse is possible if decisions require up-to-the-minute information.

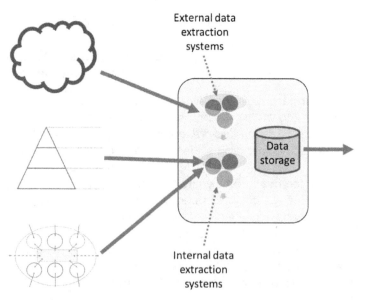

Figure 3.3 – Components of the data subsystem in a business intelligence system

Challenges in data collection

Says Colonel and NASA commander Chris Hadfield: "No astronaut launches into space with their fingers crossed. That's not how we deal with risk." All critical decisions in organizations should be made with the same stance, seeking to minimize any error or unforeseen result by analyzing all scenarios, trends, and correlations, understanding the anomalies that may arise, and thus defining possible alternatives for action. The great challenge is that an in-depth analysis will hardly be able to be carried out by a person without the help of a machine, which can find outstanding findings where the human cannot identify them with the naked eye.

Today, the primary threats to the survival of organizations and societies do not come from sudden events but from slow and gradual processes. Therefore, finding patterns, trends, correlations, and causalities between the existing variables becomes very relevant.

Most SME owners in Latin America spend more time trying to obtain information than running their businesses. According to surveys of managers and directors, 20% or more of the time is spent processing information. Therefore, in an organization working Monday to Friday, one of the five days is entirely dedicated to organizing data. The use of tools that manage to consolidate and present the information according to the company's requirements allows this effort to be minimized.

Two other essential aspects for proper data analysis are the sources of information, their automation, and the filtering and correction of the data.

According to research conducted a few years ago in the United States, the cost of erroneous data has reached 10-25% of a business's revenue, impacting more than 3 trillion dollars per year. [Colosimo, 2015]

In computer science, the term "garbage in, garbage out" is well known, referring to the fact that the more contaminated and erroneous information a database has, the more the analysis and conclusions obtained will be corrupted. Companies have to identify the risks in the process and the tools for generating information in the different departments to minimize them. Unfortunately, most organizations don't focus on reviewing, cleaning, and correcting data.

In a database, there are traditionally four types of erroneous data: duplicate data, missing information, inaccurate information, and incorrect information.

Duplicate data: refers to data that is registered two (or sometimes more) times in the database. For example, a customer buying two products and getting two different customer numbers.

Missing information: sometimes, in the records, the filling in specific fields, like age, may allow segmentation or provide more information related to the transaction. The person in charge of capturing that record may consider it optional and choose to leave it blank.

Inaccurate information: there is information that was correct when initially captured, but over time, it changed and is now erroneous—for example, a customer who changed their address and hasn't updated the database.

Incorrect Information: This is related to any incorrect data in the database (strictly speaking, inaccurate information could also be considered within this category). For example, when registered, an item's price is incorrectly specified.

Figure 3.4 - Types of erroneous data

Of the four categories, the first two are more straightforward to identify and correct than the last. Duplicate data is sometimes resolved with validations carried out in the database (for example, when creating a new register, the system should not allow it to be made if there is already a customer with the same company name or federal taxpayer number). The process is complicated when the records include certain variations in how an article description is written. Tools for preparing and cleaning data, such as OpenRefine and Tableau Prep, allow you to group similar records to obtain automatic recommendations for standardizing records that, in theory, should have the same information.

In the case of missing information, the validations to be created by the system are usually more straightforward since the system should not allow a user to leave mandatory fields blank before generating a record.

Detecting inaccurate information is usually more complicated unless the field's content is obviously incorrect (for example, someone who, instead of putting a description, puts a period only). These cases require human intervention, data review, and correction routines. Thus, depending on the possible causes of the errors (misinterpretation, mistyping of the information, or problems with interfaces to other platforms from which the information is obtained initially), it is necessary to promote training, create review routines or even some incentive (or even punishment in case of unacceptable data quality) for the validation processes.

It's important to consider that, typically, processes that are more automated and require less intervention and manipulation of data by people have less potential for errors. ERP (Enterprise Resource Planning) solutions are relevant for this since they automate the flow of information between departments, especially those with greater market penetration and protocols with international standards in their processes, such as SAP or Oracle.

According to research findings (see Figure 3.5), the best-performing companies generally invest in data management and integration, as well as data integrity processes and technology to improve quality and coordination.

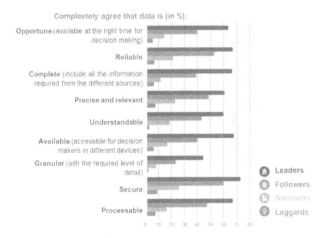

Figure 3.5 - Results of an international research by IDC about data quality [IDC, 2019]

This data is used to influence decision-making and as a source for training artificial intelligence and machine learning algorithms, a virtuous circle of positive reinforcement.

Samples in Data Analysis

In data analytics, as in statistics in general, the more information you have for analysis, the better. If we had a record of every possible variable within the universe to be analyzed, it would be said that the study would be carried out on the population. Unfortunately, that is often difficult, expensive, or even impossible. For example, if you wanted the opinion on security matters of each person within our country (or even within a specific state), it would be a titanic task, the results of which would not justify the associated investment. That is why the analysis is commonly carried out on a sample of this population, that is, only a part.

Selecting a sample requires representative items (typically in a finite population between 5% and 10% of the population data). Moreover, data collection should be random within the different types of population segments since there is a high risk of such information being biased. For example, an online survey of citizens about their perception of local government performance which ignores citizens without internet access; the results will likely be biased.

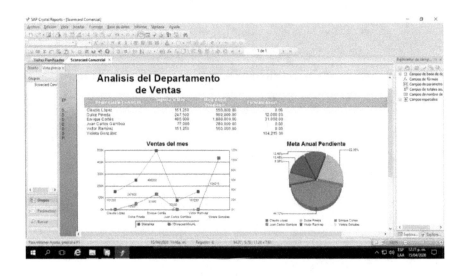

Figure 3.6 - Example of a report created with Crystal Reports

3.4.- The analysis subsystem

The analysis subsystem consists of mathematical models, tools, and computer programs that allow data to be manipulated to identify trends, statistics, or ways of presenting information to the decision-maker. It consists of the specialized hardware to process and present the information, plus the programs (software) necessary for the analysis.

Although most organizations, to a greater or lesser extent, come to use spreadsheets (mainly Excel) for the preparation of reports and graphs, there are complementary tools, such as packages for the visualization of flat reports that some administrative systems have or directly in database managers (for example, SQL Server). Others, such as Crystal Reports, are business intelligence tools with the ability to display graphical reports and develop formats, being able to classify and insert conditional formats, parameters, or groupings in the visualization, in addition to generating graphs or associated reports (nested) with each other, being able to have report-controlled access to different users (see Figure 3.6).

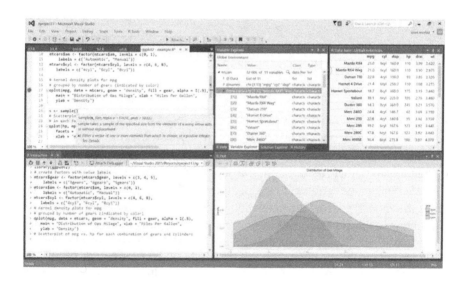

Figure 3.7 - Example of Microsoft R Open

There is also statistical analysis software, such as SPSS, Matlab, or R, that allows you to identify dispersion, correlations, central tendency, or regressions between data sets, having the option of showing results graphically (see Figure 3.7). Another software category, Data Mining, also uses statistical information to automatically discover patterns in large volumes of data and transform them into more refined information. Examples include Rapidminer and Sisense (see Figure 3.8).

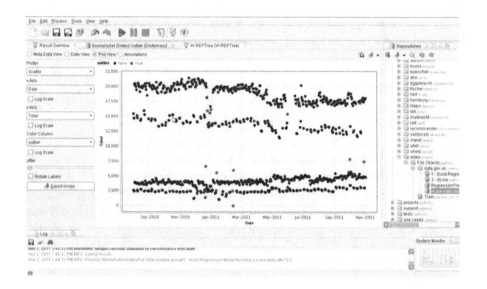

Figure 3.8 - Example of Rapidminer [Pat Research, 2021]

However, there are applications designed for a more complete and versatile analysis of information, called Business Intelligence tools (also known as Business Intelligence or BI), aimed at the development and achievement of organizational objectives through analytics and which can have a diversity of functionalities, depending on the perspectives they cover. As a definition, BI are systems that allow the collection, management, and interpretation of information, allowing its graphical analysis for decision-making.

An advantage of these tools is that they can connect to the most common databases, regardless of the administrative system in which you work, and they can simultaneously connect information from different tools (with other databases). The important thing is that the data is physically stored and structured in a database manager (which can be achieved through data modeling).

Dashboards vs Scorecards

In execution, within the descriptive analysis, it is usually essential to monitor the operation, and that is given from two different types of reports: control panels and dashboards.

A **dashboard** concentrates multiple reports, providing easy access to numerous data sets simultaneously (see Figure 3.10). Unlike scorecards, dashboards are used as a real-time monitoring tool. Data is constantly updated, allowing organizations to track their operational performance in real-time.

A **scorecard** is a means used to align the evolution of the strategy with the objectives, usually set in the medium and long term. It is excellent for evaluating the evolution of performance based on the strategy (a Key Business Indicator, or KPI) and sometimes even to identify if it is necessary to rethink the organization's strategy. It is widespread to use traffic lights for graphs or tables displayed so that if the performance is equivalent to or higher than the strategy, the current level is shown in green. If the current results are slightly lower than expected, they are displayed in yellow or orange; in case of bad results, they are in red.

Figure 3.9 - Comparison between dashboard and score card

Figure 3.10 - Example of a dashboard using SAP Analytics Cloud

Traditionally, scorecards have presented a more static view of an organization at any given time, rather than a dynamic perspective to monitor organizational progress, without allowing for real-time analysis or levels of visualization detail due to the challenges involved in the past integrating all information silos at the corporate level.

A dashboard is better for managing operations, and a scorecard is better for managing strategies. As technologies advance and more efficient handling of large amounts of data, there are more and more tools that allow us to blur the line between them with indicators that integrate the virtues of both, which could be called "strategic control panels" or "operational dashboards."

A strategic dashboard can be part of a limited and concise set of measures representing the organization's strategy. You could create a simple one-page view of these vital strategic measures while maintaining the ability to drill down and analyze the results.

An operational scorecard would offer tactical (short-term) objectives rather than strategic (long-term) ones to be applied in particular situations or projects that could manage several projects simultaneously. It's a scorecard with a more short-term focus. [Jackson, 2024; Sisense 2024]

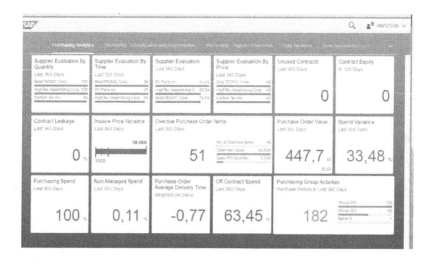

Figure 3.11 - Purchasing information using several scorecards with S/4 HANA

Creating Graphical Analysis: From Technician to End User

Previously, creating or modifying any chart in a Business Intelligence (BI) tool required the intervention of a technical specialist in the field. As has happened with many other applications, access to design on these platforms has become more accessible and more efficient, with functionalities that allow any end user to develop their own graphics without any technical knowledge and analyze their perspectives on the fly (called Cube Analysis). Examples include Tableau, Power BI, Qlik Sense, and SAP Analytics Cloud.

The Need for Big Data Analytics: Big Data

Big data refers to extensive and complex data sets that present various characteristics or challenges, represented by the so-called 4 V's: **Volume** (large amounts of data), **Velocity, Variety**, and **Veracity** of the data (some authors also include **Value** of the data as an additional "V"). It should be noted that 80% of the current data in the world has been generated in the last two years alone, which continues to occur exponentially.

These types of datasets are challenging to handle with traditional data processing tools, and because of this, there are new technologies that allow data to be processed much more efficiently.

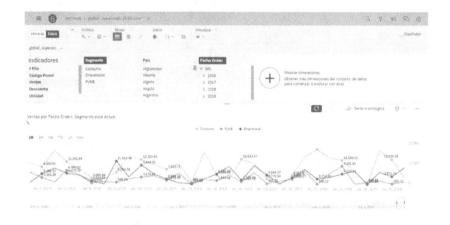

Figure 3.12 - Example of cube analysis using SAP Analytics Cloud

How difficult is it to manage and analyze the operation in an organization?

A company processes many transactions daily, perhaps hundreds, thousands, millions, or more, depending on the company's size. Let's take a Formula 1 race as an analogy, an event that lasts about an hour and a half.

On average, an F1 car carries between 150 and 300 sensors. Each team has two cars in the race, so between them, 13 billion pieces of data are generated during the race. Assuming that data was people, that's almost twice the world's population. Considering that reference data can be given in an hour and a half, everything relevant that can be measurable in an organization over a year can be much higher in volume.

Traditional data processing platforms host data for processing on the hard drive and then process it in RAM, while specific platforms specialized in the disruptive management of Big Data host data directly in RAM, which allows you to ask questions and get their answer in 100 milliseconds (1/10 of a second). This level of responsiveness enables the speed of analysis to be more than 10,000 times faster than some conventional platforms, which would be equivalent to walking from Lima, Peru, to Cancun, Mexico, in 6 minutes, allowing the consolidation of vast volumes of data efficiently, facilitating the performance of predictive analysis and the application of Artificial Intelligence algorithms within administrative systems and in Business Intelligence tools. An example of this type of Big Data processing tool is SAP HANA.

40

3.5.- From operational information to experiential information

Initially, organizations focused on the recording and analysis of operational data (called "O-Data"). Sales, deliveries, invoicing, or payments are examples of everyday operations in any company.

However, it began to be detected that some retail studies claim that 70% of purchase decisions are based on experience, so it began to lend itself to capturing experiential data (called "X-Data"), which is the one that answers the root causes of the customer's future choices or the "why." And they will most likely be able to predict their loyalty. It is not the same to have a record of the number and amount of returns in an organization for a certain period (O-Data) as the reasons that cause such a return (delay in the response, poor attention from an executive, deficiencies in the quality of the product or service or other, which constitute the X-Data).

When customers leave a mall, we wonder if they had a good experience. Conventional means to measure the expertise were limited in the application of satisfaction surveys; however, nowadays, mainly e-commerce and retail come to leverage other types of technology-based methods, such as the number of clicks a customer gives or the time spent on a website or in a physical store in facial recognition to analyze and profile the customer. Evaluate their average purchases or use heat maps to recognize traffic and movement in different store parts.

It's a game changer to consider that some statistics show that 80% of managers believe they deliver a superior customer experience, while only 8% of customers agree.

3.6.- Ethics and regulations in data handling

Human beings are beings of habits, so if you look closely at their past behavior, it is possible to understand their tastes and project their behaviors. The Internet, computers, mobile devices, wearables (such as smartwatches), and more and more technological tools record and process the footprint of your actions to help provide you with recommendations for apps, readings, routines, movies, videos, and music, among many other things. At the same time, this makes it easier to exploit and vulnerable to advertisers and other providers. Information has now become the most valuable commodity over what was traditionally considered oil, leading to an ethical dilemma in properly handling data. In the most severe cases, it has even caused multiple scandals and complaints, such as that of Facebook for having inappropriately shared the data of 87 million users with the consulting firm Cambridge Analytica, which resulted in a record fine of 5 billion dollars. [BBC News World, 2019]

For this reason, there is an increasing tightening and regulation of privacy and data protection within organizations, in relationships with customers and suppliers (including auditing firms), and on the Internet.

On the other hand, scandals that occurred around the year 2000 regarding the valuation of companies listed on the stock exchange as a whole (including one of the leading consulting firms of the time, Arthur Andersen) caused the development of the Sarbanes Oxley Act (SOX) in the United States, to which the financial information of any organization with operations in that country must adhere. That reports or is listed on the New York Stock Exchange. This law has regulated various controls in the United States to improve the quality of financial information based on accounting standards, internal control, corporate governance, audit independence, and increased penalties for financial crimes, allowing, among other things, to identify and evaluate the impact of key financial information risks on organizations.

Minicase - The Cost of Not Keeping a Secret

In 2010, Facebook launched the Open Graph, a way for app developers to view Facebook user data. In 2013, an app called "thisisyourdigitallife" enrolled 300,000 Facebook users but also obtained information from its subscribers' contacts. Reports indicate that the company may have obtained data from millions of users without their consent. In 2014, Facebook changed the rules to make consent necessary, but it didn't make it retroactive. Cambridge Analytica, a political consulting firm, allegedly used that data to target advertising campaigns in the U.S. election. The scandal became public in 2018. After a nearly year-long investigation, Facebook agrees to pay a $5 billion fine (without admitting fault). [Meredith, 2018; Davies & Rushe, 2019]

3.7.- Summary

- From a functional point of view, a business intelligence system comprises three main components: the data subsystem, the analytics subsystem, and the user.
- The data subsystem collects, cleans, and stores the information for decisions. The information can come from sources inside or outside the company.
- There are four types of erroneous data: duplicate data, missing information, inaccurate information, and incorrect information.
- The analysis subsystem consists of mathematical models, tools, and computer programs that allow data to be manipulated to identify trends, statistics, or ways of presenting information to the decision-maker.
- Information analysis tools can be based on total information (population) or random (unbiased) representative samples.
- Business Intelligence tools can have three main analytical perspectives: descriptive, predictive, and prescriptive.
- A dashboard concentrates multiple reports that provide easy access to various data sets simultaneously. They are used as a real-time monitoring tool.
- A scorecard is a means used to align the evolution of the strategy with the objectives. Traditionally, they present a more static view of an organization at any given time.
- Big data (also translated as "big data") refers to large and complex data sets that present various characteristics or challenges, represented by the so-called 4 V's: Volume (large volumes of data), Velocity, Variety, and Veracity of the data (there are authors who also include Value of the data as an additional "V").
- There is an increasing tightening and regulation of privacy and data protection within organizations in relationships with customers and suppliers.
- The Sarbanes Oxley Act (SOX), mandatory for the financial reporting of any organization with operations in the U.S., regulates various controls to improve the quality of financial reporting.

3.8.- Review exercises

Questions

1. What impact does misinformation have on businesses?
2. How much is the cost of misinformation estimated?
3. What are the four types of erroneous data?
4. What is the difference between population and sample?
5. What characteristics must a sample have to represent an entire population?
6. Mention some tools for data analysis
7. What is the difference between descriptive, predictive, and prescriptive analytics?
8. What is the difference between a dashboard and a scorecard?
9. What is big data?
10. What are the four (or five) V's of big data?
11. Where did the Sarbanes Oxley Act (SOX) come from, and what is it for?

Exercises

1. Research a data analysis tool and visit the tool's website. What does the tool do? What is it used for? Name some actual users of the tool.
2. Research some applications of Big Data in industry.

Module II

Valuation and Prioritization of
Business Intelligence Projects

Chapter 4

Analysis of Costs and Benefits of a Technology Project

> *"Managers and investors alike must understand that accounting numbers are the beginning, not the end, of business valuation."*
>
> Warren Buffett, "Chairman's letter", 1983.

4.1.- Learning objectives

- Identify the costs and benefits of a business intelligence project.
- Distinguish between tangible and intangible costs and benefits.
- Understanding the concept of marginal costs and benefits.
- Identify ways to present the cost-benefit information of a business intelligence project.

4.2.- How do you determine if a proposal represents a good project or a bad project?

An IT consultant is proposing to install a new customer relationship management system for an insurance company. The company must invest in the software, and in building the interfaces between the new system and the ERP that is already installed. In addition, the insurance company must purchase new computer equipment because the one it has would not be powerful enough to operate the proposed system. It also needs to train the entire sales force in the use of the new system.

The decision to approve or not approve a project depends on many factors. It's not just based on the cost of the software. However, if the project were to be so expensive that it was not within the company's reach, there is no other decision than to reject it and look for a solution more in line with the possibilities of the business.

Assuming the company had the money to pay for the project, the next question is: what benefits does it bring? And how complicated is it to get the project to work? A project that costs dearly and does not produce profits is easy to reject. Similarly, projects that wouldn't work are also quickly rejected.

Analyzing whether a project is suitable for an organization requires calculating its costs (both tangible and intangible) and its benefits (tangible and intangible), as well as the risk involved in its implementation. This should be done for a period equivalent to the life of the project (so if the project is expected to serve for five years, the costs and benefits should be calculated over that entire period). With this information, it is easier to decide whether the new system should be approved or not.

4.3.- Costs of a project

The cost of a project involves the direct outlays of money to pay for something and the losses due to not gaining something by doing the project. Direct expenses include start-up costs (to purchase the equipment and software) and operating costs (to operate it during its useful life). There are indirect costs, which are costs or losses incurred by not doing something typically done instead of working on the project. Suppose a salesperson is required to attend a one-day training course. In that case, the cost of that training is not only the money spent on training materials and the instructor but also the money lost from sales not made because the workforce was attending the course.

Some examples of costs to consider are:

Project start-up costs:

- Hardware
- Software
- Consulting
- Converting data from the old system to the new system
- Cost of Training Courses

Project Operating Costs:

- Hardware Maintenance
- Software Maintenance
- Communications & Operating Costs
- Additional staff needed to operate the project

Indirect costs:

- Cost of staff participating in training courses
- Other losses that can be attributed to a project
- Length of time the data center must be out of service while the new equipment is being installed
- Sales not made by sales staff while in training courses instead of selling
- Problems in operation as staff acclimate to the new system

Minicase - Hidden Costs

The automobile is a symbol of freedom. There's nothing like knowing you can get in the car and travel anywhere, anytime. However, in some cities, people, even with much money, choose not to own a car. The argument for using taxis in certain towns is that the parking spaces sometimes cost more than vehicles.

When you buy a car, your monthly expenses go up. Not only do you have to pay for the vehicle, but you also have to pay for license plates and taxes, maintenance, gas, insurance, and even a parking space. If a person only plans to use the car for 20 minutes daily to get to and from work, will it be more convenient to have a car, or is it better to use taxis?

4.4.- Benefits of a project

Like costs, benefits can come from revenue (such as a sale) or savings (such as reducing travel expenses by being able to do business online). While some benefits can be identified immediately at the start of a project, most of the benefits are reflected over the project's life. Some examples of the benefits of a project could be:

Benefits at the start of a project

- Savings from Shutting Down an Obsolete Data Center
- Reduction in equipment maintenance costs (by using new equipment)

Benefits over the life of the project

- Increase in sales
- Reduction in the company's operating costs
- Reduction in travel expenses
- Reduction in the workforce

4.5.- Intangible costs and benefits

Sometimes, a project provides certain benefits that are not immediately quantifiable. For example, a new system can make the company look modern or make employees happier using the latest technology. In the same way, a new system can provoke dissatisfaction in people who already know the old system and prefer not to risk trying a new model.

Intangible costs and benefits cannot be quantified (priced in dollars and cents) but must be mentioned to be taken into account when deciding whether or not to approve a project. In social organizations or in government, where the leading indicator of success is not how much money is earned, some projects can be justified by the value to society or by the image they provide.

Typically, a project is justified regarding its tangible costs and benefits. The intangible costs and benefits serve as the "decoration on the cake." If you resort to intangible benefits to justify an organization's projects, eventually, the company will cease to be profitable and go out of business. If the company has to close because it is unaffordable, there is no point in having the best public image or the happiest employees.

Some intangible benefits provide long-term benefits. Better decisions can eventually produce higher income, although it is difficult to attribute an income to a particular decision. Transaction processing systems that improve processes or eliminate labor are simpler to justify, based on their tangible benefits than management and decision support systems [Laudon & Laudon, 2020].

In Mexico, everyone will one day have to use the services of the Civil Registry. One of the most used services is requesting copies of birth certificates. The process typically takes two days; the user goes to the office to ask for a certificate and pays for the service. The documents are prepared that afternoon, and the user can pick them up the next day. A system to streamline the process so that the certificates can be issued when requested (requiring only one visit by the user) would require a significant investment in equipment, data capture, and software. Being more efficient would not increase the number of certificates people request or reduce the personnel cost in the offices that issue the certificates. The benefit is that people only need one visit to get their documents, and the government generates an image of modernity and customer service. Is it justifiable to invest in modernizing the Civil Registry?

4.6.- Marginal costs and benefits

If a new online sales platform helps sell $1,200,000 worth of products, but with the current one, the company already sells $1,000,000, the new system only provides a $200,000 profit in upsells. If the company decides not to implement the project, it will already have sales of one million dollars. The marginal benefit is the additional benefit to what you already have. In this case, when calculating the project's sales profit, it only brings in $200,000, not $1,200,000.

Similarly, if the company already has a computer or pays rent for an office and the new system occupies the same equipment (if no additional equipment needs to be purchased) and does not require additional space, the cost of equipment and office rent for the project is zero, because the company, if it decides not to approve the project, would still have to spend those amounts.

On the other hand, if the software can run on the current computer but needs a $100,000 memory expansion, the equipment cost for the project is not the cost of the computer you already have but just the additional 100,000 that would have to be paid to run the software.

Marginal costs are those additional costs to those already required to carry out a project. A project is analyzed solely in terms of its marginal costs and benefits.

4.7.- Tabulating Cash Flows from Technology Projects

A relatively easy way to understand and present the costs and benefits of a project is to use a timetable to show the project's cash flows (money inflows and outflows). The lifespan of a project can be divided into years, quarters, or months (depending on the expected scope). The names of the costs to be tabulated are placed in the left column and the periods in the top row. The expense incurred or benefit received for each item in each period is placed in each cell.

There may be line items with subtotals of costs incurred and benefits received. The last line lists the flow of each period obtained by subtracting the costs from the benefits.

Table 4.1.- Tabulation of a new project's cash flows

	1	2	3	4	5	6	7	8	9	10	Total
Marginal costs											
remodeling	30000	10000									
equipment	10000	30000									
legal requirements	10000										
operation	5000	5000	2000	2000	2000	2000	2000	2000	2000	2000	
total costs	55000	45000	2000	2000	2000	2000	2000	2000	2000	2000	116000
Marginal Benefits											
sales	0	8000	20000	20000	20000	20000	20000	20000	20000	20000	
travel expenses	0	0	1500	3000	3000	3000	3000	3000	3000	3000	
total benefits	0	8000	21500	23000	23000	23000	23000	23000	23000	23000	190500
net flow	-55000	-37000	19500	21000	21000	21000	21000	21000	21000	21000	
accumulated flow	-55000	-92000	-72500	-51500	-30500	-9500	11500	32500	53500	74500	74500

4.8.- What level of detail is necessary when calculating the costs and benefits of a project?

In most cases, whether a project is profitable can be determined by analyzing the most significant costs and benefits. It is common for the cost of hardware, software, maintenance, and consulting to account for a substantial percentage of the total. Of course, the project may require printer ink, paper, and electricity. Still, those costs are usually so small that whether they are added to an analysis table will have little effect on the final decision.

Similarly, the benefits to consider are usually only the most significant items. In a typical project, increases in sales, personnel savings, and reductions in maintenance costs would account for the bulk of the benefits to be realized.

Therefore, a table with ten to twelve lines between the costs and benefits of a project may be enough to know whether a project is profitable or not. Except for exceptional cases where detail is critical, the time and effort involved in obtaining estimated details of each cost element and each expected profit point are generally not justified in terms of better decisions.

4.9.- Summary

- Analyzing whether a project suits an organization requires calculating its costs (tangible and intangible), benefits (tangible and intangible), and the risks involved in its implementation.
- The project cost involves the direct outlays of money to pay for something and the losses due to not gaining something by doing the project.
- Like costs, benefits can come from revenue (such as a sale) or savings (such as reducing travel expenses by being able to do business online).
- Intangible costs and benefits cannot be quantified (priced in dollars and cents) but must be mentioned to be taken into account when deciding whether or not to approve a project.
- Typically, a project is justified regarding its tangible costs and benefits. If you resort to intangible benefits to justify many of an organization's projects, eventually, the company will cease to be profitable and go out of business.
- Marginal costs are those additional costs to those already required to carry out a project. A project is analyzed solely in terms of its marginal costs and benefits.

4.10.- Review exercises

Questions

1. What is a tangible benefit?
2. What is a tangible cost?
3. Why are expense savings considered benefits?
4. What are intangible benefits?
5. What are marginal costs and benefits?
6. Why is it that only marginal costs and benefits are used when analyzing the profitability of a project?

Exercises

1. Identify the costs and benefits of having an ATM in a bank.
2. Identify the most significant costs and benefits for a sports store of opening a website to sell their products there.
3. Look for a project that isn't profitable and explain why it's not.
4. Identify a project with more costs than benefits implemented in an organization and explain why it was accepted.
5. List some tangible benefits of using an ERP in a company.
6. List some tangible costs of implementing a CRM system in an organization.

Chapter 5

Quantitative Project Analysis

"Remember that Time is Money. He that can earn Ten Shillings a Day by his Labour, and goes abroad, or sits idle one half of that Day, tho' he spends but Sixpence during his Diversion or Idleness, ought not to reckon That the only Expence; he has really spent or rather thrown away Five Shillings besides.
Remember that Credit is Money. If a Man lets his Money lie in my Hands after it is due, he gives me the Interest, or so much as I can make of it during that Time. This amounts to a considerable Sum where a Man has good and large Credit, and makes good Use of it."

Benjamin Franklin, "Advice to a young tradesman, written by an old one," 1748.

5.1.- Learning objectives

- Know the concept of the value of money over time.
- Be able to identify and analyze cash flows.
- Learn how to calculate future value (FV) and present value (PV).
- Understand the concept of Minimum Acceptable Rate of Return (MARR).
- Know how to compute the net present value of an investment.
- Know how to estimate the internal rate of return of an investment project.
- Be able to interpret the results of investment evaluations.

5.2.- The value of money over time

Money, if invested wisely, yields interest. If I deposit 100 dollars in the bank, in an account that pays an interest rate of 10% per year, at the end of a year, I will have 110 dollars. If my business is to sell fruit, and a hundred dollars of fruit brings me a profit of fifteen dollars in one year, then the return on my fruit investment is 15%.

Therefore, receiving a hundred dollars today differs from a hundred dollars one year from now. If someone pays me a hundred dollars today, I can invest them (in the bank or my fruit business) and have, within a year, more than the hundred with which I started. If one project pays me a hundred dollars today and another offers me a hundred dollars one year from now, the one that pays me today would be a better deal. One hundred and ten dollars in one year would be equivalent to one hundred today (considering that I can invest them in an account that pays 10% annually). If I have to compare a business that offers me 100 dollars today against one that gives me 120 dollars in a year, and my options are to invest the money at 10% per year, then 120 dollars in a year is better than 100 today.

As Benjamin Franklin said in 1748, "If a Man lets his Money lie in my Hands after it is due, he gives me the Interest, or so much as I can make of it during that Time." [Franklin, 1748]

At today's price, money is known as money at present value. The amount of money you will have at some point in the future is known as future value. Considering a rate of return (or interest) of 10% per annum, the future value of one hundred dollars in one year is one hundred and ten dollars. In the same way, the present value of one hundred and ten dollars in a year, at the same interest, is equivalent to one hundred dollars at present value.

5.3.- Cash flows

Another essential concept is the idea of cash flows. Money can come into the company or out of the company. An amount of money coming in is represented by a different sign than the money going out of the organization.

In this way, an investment in a bank account has a positive flow (when the money enters the account) and a negative flow (when the money is withdrawn). The cash flows can be represented on a timeline, as shown in Figure 5.1. The variable "r" represents the interest rate payable per period (in this case, 10%), "n" is the number of periods to be invested (for this example, is a single period), the inflow is the amount of the initial deposit "p" represents the present value of the investment. The outflow amount (on the right) represented by "f" is the future value of the investment after the "n" periods. Note that the amount that comes out of the account is higher than the amount that comes in, as it includes the interest generated by the investment.

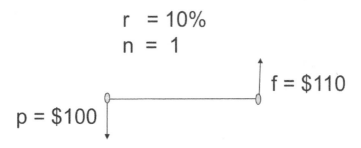

Figure 5.1 – Cash Flow in one period

If I deposit 100 dollars for three years in an account that earns 10% annual interest, how much money will I have at the end of the third year? The transaction is represented graphically in Figure 5.2

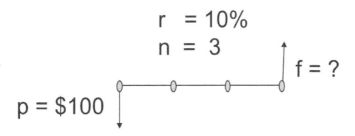

Figure 5.2 – Cash Flow in three periods

The calculation of the result gets complicated when several periods are included because the interest received on the money in the first period can also be invested and generate more interest. Therefore, the final balance of 100 dollars over three years at 10% per annum is not 130. It's 130 plus the interest generated by that interest. Table 5.1 shows the calculation of interest over three years.

If the account starts with 100 dollars and receives 10 dollars of interest in the first year, at the end of the first year, you would have 110 dollars. The second year starts with 110 dollars, and 10% of that amount is 11 dollars, so at the end of the second year, you would have 121 dollars. If the third year starts with 121 dollars, that year's interest is 12.1 dollars, so the account balance at the end of the third year would be 133.1 dollars. Therefore, the final balance of 100 dollars at 10% per annum for three years is 133.1 dollars.

Table 5.1 – Interest calculation for a three-year period

Starting balance	Interest paid	Ending balance
100	10	110
110	11	121
121	12.1	133.1

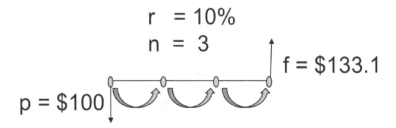

Figure 5.3 – Future value in three years

5.4.- Calculating the future and present value of money
Future Value

When calculating the future value of money, it is necessary to know the present amount of money (present value), the interest rate paid per period (interest), and the number of periods that will be considered. As stated in the previous section, one hundred dollars at 10% per annum for one year equals one hundred and ten dollars. So, the future value of 100 dollars at 10% per annum for one year is 110.

The formula for calculating future value is [Baca Urbina, 2015]:

$$F = P(1 + r)^n$$

Where:

F = future value of the investment in period n

P = present value

r = interest rate per period

n = number of periods

The formula to calculate the future value of 100 dollars at 10% per annum for three years uses the following values:

P = 100

r = 10% (in numerical terms, 10% is 0.1)

n = 3

The formula reads:

$$F = 100 \, (\, 1 + 0.1 \,)^3$$

The result is 133.1 (the same amount when calculating interest in the table). Therefore, the future value is 133.1

If the interest rate had been 5% per annum, The value of "r" would have to be replaced with 0.05 (note that 5% is 0.05 while 50% is 0.5), and the result would have been F = 115.76

Some points to watch out for formulas:

One of the most common errors in interpreting future value formulas is representing percentages numerically. 10% is represented as 0.10, 50% is represented as 0.50, 5% is 0.05, 1% is 0.01, and 100% is 1.00

The second most common error is in the interpretation of periods. Suppose the bank offers an interest rate of 10% annually, but the interest is calculated and paid monthly. In that case, the interest per month is not 10%. It is 1/12 of the annual amount, so the monthly interest is 0.833% (0.00833). The value of "n" should be adjusted to months, so "n" for one year is 12. Both the periods and the interest rates should be on the same scale.

Present Value

If you want to compare different offers, each with a different delivery date, you need to calculate how much they are equivalent to present value (or today's price) and decide which one is leaving the most profit. For example, if someone offers 100 dollars today or 120 dollars a year from now, you need to calculate the present value of both options and decide which one is better.
As with future value, to calculate present value, you need to know the expected interest rate per period and the number of periods. Solving for "P" from the future value formula defined in the previous section shows that the formula for calculating the present value of an amount of money in a certain period is [Baca Urbina, 2015]:

$$P = \frac{F}{(1 + r)^n}$$

Where:

P = present value

F = future value of the investment in period n

i = interest rate per period

n = number of periods

The present value of 100 dollars today is 100 dollars. But the present value of 120 dollars in a year is:

$$P = \frac{120}{(1 + 0.1)^1} = 109.09$$

Therefore, the offer of 120 dollars in a year is equivalent to 109.09 dollars today. That's better than 100 dollars today so that the second option would be more convenient.

If the offer had been 120 dollars in two years, the resulting present value would have been 99.17 (using the same formula, but with n=2), which would have been inconvenient.

Using Excel to Calculate the Value of Money Over Time
Excel has some functions that take data and return the result of applying the function to the provided data. The most basic functions are sum, average, count, etc.

All functions have a standard format: the equals sign followed by the name of the function followed by the entry in parentheses.

The input for a function can be:

- A set of numbers - for example, =average(2, 3, 4, 5)
  - This tells Excel to calculate the average of these numbers.
- A reference to the cell(s) - for example, =average(B1:B8) or =average(B1, B2, B3, B4, B5, B6, B7, B8)
  - This instructs Excel to calculate the average of the data that appears in all cells from B1 to B8.
  - You can type these cell references by hand or by clicking and dragging to select the cells with your mouse.

Examples of some functions are:

- =Sum(num1, num2,...) - The sum of a data group
- =Average(num1, num2,...) - the average of that data
- =Count(val1, val2,...) - the number of cells in a group containing numbers
- =Countif(range, criterion) - the number of cells in a group that meet the condition listed in the criterion

If you are using a version of Excel in a different language, the functions would have the same format, but the function names would be different depending on the language.

Using Excel to Calculate Future Value

The function used to calculate the future value of a quantity is FV for Future Value. The formula has the following format [Microsoft, 2024-1]:

FV(rate, nper, payment, [pv], [type])

The syntax of the VF function has the following arguments:

- **Rate**   Required. The interest rate per period.
- **Nper**   Required. The total number of payment periods in an annuity.
- **Pmt**   Required. The payment made each period; it cannot change over the life of the annuity. Typically, pmt contains principal and interest but no other fees or taxes. If pmt is omitted, you must include the pv argument.
- **Pv**   Optional. The present value, or the lump-sum amount that a series of future payments is worth right now (in the present). If pv is omitted, it is assumed to be 0 (zero), and you must include the pmt argument.
- **Type**   Optional. The number 0 or 1 and indicates when payments are due (0 at the end of the period, 1 at the beginning). If type is omitted, it is assumed to be 0.

The VF function calculates the future value of an investment based on a constant interest rate. The function can additionally make the calculations considering constant periodic payments or with a single fixed sum.

For example, to know the future value of 100 at 10% interest for three years, the formula would be written as follows: =FV(10%, 3, 0, 100) indicating that the interest is 10% for three periods, without additional deposits, starting with 100 dollars.

You will notice that the result is negative; if the deposit to the account is positive, Excel assumes that the future value is the amount withdrawn from the account (so it would have a different sign).

Using Excel to Calculate Present Value (Current Value)

The function used to calculate the present value of a number is PV for Present Value. The formula has the following format [Microsoft 2024-2]:

PV(rate, nper, payment, [fv], [type])

The PV function syntax has the following arguments:

- **Rate**   Required. The interest rate per period.
- **Nper**   Required. The total number of payment periods in an annuity.
- **Pmt**   Required. The payment made each period and cannot change over the life of the annuity.
- **Fv**   Optional. The future value, or a cash balance you want to attain after the last payment. If fv is omitted, it is assumed to be 0 (the future value of a loan, for example, is 0).
- **Type**   Optional. The number 0 or 1 and indicates when payments are due (0 at the end of the period, 1 at the beginning). If type is omitted, it is assumed to be 0.

The PV function calculates the present value of an investment based on a constant interest rate. The function can additionally make the calculations considering constant periodic payments or with a single fixed sum.

For example, to know the present value of 120 received in year 3 considering the 10% annual interest, the formula would be written as follows: =PV(10%, 3, 0, 120) indicating that the interest is 10%, for 3 periods, with no additional deposits.

5.5.- Minimum Acceptable Rate of Return (MARR)

Every investor (person or company) aims to profit from investment projects. The investor typically has a base rate of return against which to compare investment opportunities. This reference rate becomes the point of comparison between investments. If a project does not produce at least a rate of return equal to or greater than the baseline, the project is rejected.

This base rate is called the Minimum Acceptable Rate of Return (MARR). The MARR is a base return that would be obtained for investing under normal conditions, with much certainty and minimal risk. For example, investing in a certificate of deposit in a bank can be considered a base return, as it carries no risk. However, other investment alternatives with minimal or acceptable risks in specific industries can be used for comparison. For example, a construction company can invest money in building houses and selling them. In that case, the MARR for that type of business would be the return from the money invested in a construction project.

Many companies already know a number that they consider acceptable in their industry; in those cases, it is advisable to ask the finance area what the MARR is for projects in that organization.

If you don't have a number, it can be defined as the return on a term investment plus a premium for the risk involved in the project. If a project produces the same return as an investment in the bank, it is still more convenient to use the bank because it does not require work or involve risk. How much more than the bank does a project have to pay for to be convenient? That depends on the risk and effort required for the project to succeed. Projects requiring little risk need a premium or profit slightly higher than the bank's. In contrast, complicated projects, which involve a lot of work or risk, must produce a much higher return than the bank's return to be attractive.

5.6.- Net Present Value (NPV)

Suppose you receive an investment proposal: Make an initial investment of $1,000 in exchange for receiving cash flows over the next five years in the following amounts: year 1, $260; Year 2, $350; year 3, $480; Year 4, $325; and year 5, $275. The flows are shown in Figure 5.4

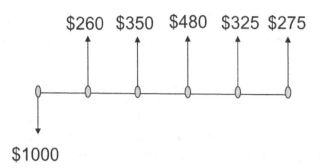

Figure 5.4 – Cash flows of an investment proposal

Deciding whether an investment is attractive requires bringing all the flows to present value and identifying whether the amount received is equivalent, at current prices, to the amount invested. All the flows are brought to present value; they are added together, and if the sum is positive, the flows are higher than the money invested, in which case the investment is convenient. If the result is negative, accepting the project would result in losses compared to investing the money at the minimum acceptable rate of return (MARR).

The sum of the present values of all the flows of an investment discounted at a specific interest rate is known as the Net Present Value.

The formula for calculating the net present value of an investment is [Baca Urbina, 2015]:

$$NPV = - CF_0 + \frac{CF_1}{(1 + r)^1} + \frac{CF_2}{(1 + r)^2} + \ldots + \frac{CF_n}{(1 + r)^n}$$

Where:

- **CFn** = net cash flow for year n, corresponding to net profit after tax in year n.
- **CFo** = initial investment in year zero.
- **r** = reference rate corresponding to the MARR.

Assuming that the MARR for this case is 10%, the resulting formula would be:

$$NPV = - 1{,}000 + 236.36 + 289.26 + 360.63 + 221.98 + 170.75$$

$$NPV = 278.98$$

In this case, for a 10% MARR, the present value of the investment is positive, which means that this project is 278.98 better than the investment alternative generated by the MARR. This project is equivalent to earning 278.98 over the alternative today.

On the other hand, if MARR were 25%, the NPV would be -99.01. A negative value means that the project is less convenient than continuing with the alternative generated by the MARR. So, while for one investor, the project may prove to be an attractive bet, for another, it could represent losses against other options they already have.

When using Excel, you can calculate the present value of each item separately and add it up using the =PV function. However, there is an alternative to calculating the net present value of a series of flows in a single equation.

To perform the calculation, add the value of the interest rate plus the current value of the flows for each period with the formula =NPV Excel.

The syntax of the NPV formula is as follows [Microsoft, 2024-3]:

NPV(rate; value1; [value2];...)

The syntax of the NPV function has the following arguments:

- **Rate**   Required. The rate of discount over the length of one period.
- **Value1, value2,...**   Value1 is required; subsequent values are optional. 1 to 254 arguments representing the payments and income. Value1; value2;... They must be of the same duration and occur at the end of each period.

In the case of the example in this section, the flows are placed on one line, occupying one column each. The formula for calculating net present value is =+A1+NPV(0.1, B1:F1).

A1 is already at present value; adding the net present value of cells B1 to F1 with a discount rate (interest) of 10% (which is written as 0.1) yields the project's net present value.

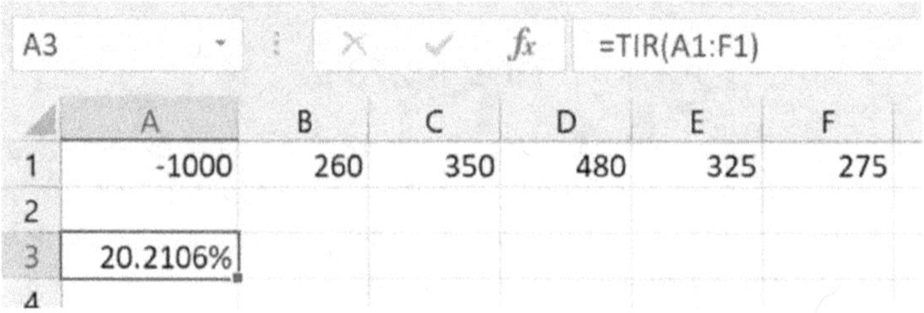

A3			f_x	=TIR(A1:F1)		
	A	B	C	D	E	F
1	-1000	260	350	480	325	275
2						
3	20.2106%					
4						

Figure 5.5.- Calculating the net present value of some cash flows using Excel.

To be careful:

- The signs in each cell are essential: an expense or investment is written as a negative number, and an income is positive.
- Each column represents a period. If you don't receive income in one period, it's imperative to fill that space with a zero. Otherwise, Excel can assume that the following year's flow occurs in the year with no value.
- Decimals represent percentages in numerical form. 10% is written 0.10; 5% is written 0.05; 50% is written 0.50.
- The discount rate (or interest rate) is the same for all periods and is for the entire period. If the period is monthly but the reference rate is by an annual percentage, then the rate to be captured in the formula should be the yearly rate divided by 12.
- Payments are assumed to occur at the end of each period.

5.7.- Internal rate of return (IRR)

In the example in the previous section, two cases were studied: an investor with a 10% AR and another with a 25% ARR. Let's assume there are five investors, each with a different MARR: (10%, 15%, 20%, 25%, and 30%). When calculating the NPV of the investment for each investor, it is found that for three of them, the investment is acceptable, while for the two highest, the investment is not. Table 5.2 shows the results.

Table 5.2 - Variations in the value of the NPV for different MARR

Investor	MARR	NPV
A	10%	$278.98
B	15%	$128.89
C	20%	$4.75
D	25%	-$99.01
E	30%	-$186.56

This table shows that the project is profitable compared to a discount rate of 20%, while against 25%, it is not. Therefore, this project gives a discount rate between 20 and 25 percent.

The exact interest rate obtained from the project is called the Internal Rate of Return (IRR). Calculating the IRR requires finding the interest rate to make the net present value zero.

In the NPV formula, the following equation should be solved for "i":

$$0 = - CF_0 + \frac{CF_1}{(1 + r)^1} + \frac{CF_2}{(1 + r)^2} + \cdots + \frac{CF_n}{(1 + r)^n}$$

Solving the equation for "i" would be an extremely complicated job, so an alternative would be to arrive at the result by multiple approximations, trying different values of i until the solution is found. Another way is plotting the NPV for various "i" values and finding the point on the graph where the NPV intercepts zero. The third alternative is to use technology.

Excel has a function to calculate the value for "i" of a series of flows. The feature is called IRR.

The syntax of the IRR formula is as follows [Microsoft, 2021-4]:

IRR(values, [estimate])

The syntax of the IRR function has the following arguments:

- **Values**   Required. It is an array or a reference to cells that contain the numbers for which you want to calculate the internal rate of return.
  - The values argument must contain at least one positive and one negative value to calculate the internal rate of return.
  - IRR interprets the order of cash flows following the order of the values argument. Be sure to enter the values of the payments and revenues in the correct order.
- **Estimate**   Optional. This is a number that the user estimates will approximate the IRR result.
  - Microsoft Excel uses an iterative technique for IRR calculation. From the number placed as an estimate, IRR

cycles through the calculation until the result has an accuracy of 0.00001 percent. If IRR can't find a working result after 20 attempts, the error value #NUM is returned.
- o In most cases, you do not need to provide the estimate argument for the IRR calculation. If you omit the estimate argument, it is assumed to be 0.1 (10%).
- o If IRR returns #NUM, or if the result doesn't come close to your expected value, try again with a different value for estimation.

In this case, the formula used =IRR(A1:F1) includes all flows in the project. An estimate was not included, and Excel starts by default with 0.1 (10%).

A3			f_x	=+IRR(A1:F1)		
	A	B	C	D	E	F
1	-1000	260	350	480	325	275
2						
3	20.2106%					
4						

Figure 5.6.- Calculating the IRR of some cash flows using Excel.

This result says that investing in this project is equivalent to putting money in the bank at an interest rate of 20.2106% per annum (closer to 20% than 25%, as seen in Table 5.2). Therefore, if the resulting IRR is better than the proposed MARR, the project is acceptable, while if it is less than the MARR, the project is rejected.

To be careful:

- The IRR function requires at least one positive and one negative number to exist in the list to work. An investment with only positive flows is infinitely profitable (with a zero investment, you get a profit). Similarly, an investment that only has negative flows is infinitely unprofitable.
- The resulting IRR is the interest per period. If each column represents a month, the resulting IRR is monthly (to obtain the annual interest, you would have to multiply it by 12). If each column represents a year, the resulting IRR is annual.
- Sometimes, the cell where the IRR is calculated is formatted with few decimal places or integers; it is critical to extend the number of decimal places where the answer will appear to ensure that you see an accurate result.

5.8.- Interpreting investment valuations

Based on the example developed in Chapter 4, where the costs and benefits of an IT project are analyzed, an analysis of the net present value and the internal rate of return can be carried out. In the alternative presented, as initially proposed, in year one, an investment of $55,000 is required, and no benefits are received; in the second year, there is an expense of $45,000, but benefits equivalent to $8000 are received. In the following years, expenses decreased to as little as $2,000, and benefits increased in year three to $12,500 and from year four onwards by $14,000.

Finding the project's IRR requires adding a line with the net flow of each period. The net flow is calculated by adding the income and subtracting the expenses for each period. So, the flow of year 1 is -55,000, and that of year 6 (for example) is $12,000.

Based on the assumption that the MARR for the company is 10%, the formula for calculating the NPV is =B16+IRR(B18, C16:K16), and the formula for calculating the IRR is =IRR(B16:K16,0)

In this case, the results are a NPV of -$31,676.84 and an IRR of 0.5229%. This result is much lower than the expected MARR (10%), so this project, as presented, would be rejected.

		1	2	3	4	5	6	7	8	9	10
4											
5	Marginal costs										
6	remodeling	30,000	10,000								
7	equipment	10,000	30,000								
8	legal requirements	10,000									
9	operation	5,000	5,000	2,000	2,000	2,000	2,000	2,000	2,000	2,000	2,000
10	total costs	55,000	45,000	2,000	2,000	2,000	2,000	2,000	2,000	2,000	2,000
11	Marginal Benefits										
12	sales	-	8,000	11,000	11,000	11,000	11,000	11,000	11,000	11,000	11,000
13	travel expenses	-	-	1,500	3,000	3,000	3,000	3,000	3,000	3,000	3,000
14	total benefits	-	8,000	12,500	14,000	14,000	14,000	14,000	14,000	14,000	14,000
15											
16	net flow	- 55,000	- 37,000	10,500	12,000	12,000	12,000	12,000	12,000	12,000	12,000
17	accumulated flow	- 55,000	- 92,000	- 81,500	- 69,500	- 57,500	- 45,500	- 33,500	- 21,500	- 9,500	2,500
18											
19	MARR rate	10.000%		Mimimum rate required by the company							
20	Net Present Value	-31,676.84		Project's value compared with putting the money in the bank							
21	Internal Rate of Return	0.5229%		Interest rate that the project is paying							

Figure 5.7 - Financial analysis of an investment project

	1	2	3	4	5	6	7	8	9	10
5 **Marginal costs**										
6 remodeling	30,000	10,000								
7 equipment	10,000	30,000								
8 legal requirements	10,000									
9 operation	5,000	5,000	2,000	2,000	2,000	2,000	2,000	2,000	2,000	2,000
10 total costs	55,000	45,000	2,000	2,000	2,000	2,000	2,000	2,000	2,000	2,000
11 **Marginal Benefits**										
12 sales	-	8,000	22,000	22,000	22,000	22,000	22,000	22,000	22,000	22,000
13 travel expenses	-	-	1,500	3,000	3,000	3,000	3,000	3,000	3,000	3,000
14 total benefits	-	8,000	23,500	25,000	25,000	25,000	25,000	25,000	25,000	25,000
15										
16 net flow	- 55,000	- 37,000	21,500	23,000	23,000	23,000	23,000	23,000	23,000	23,000
17 accumulated flow	- 55,000	- 92,000	- 70,500	- 47,500	- 24,500	- 1,500	21,500	44,500	67,500	90,500

19 MARR rate	10.000%	Mimimum rate required by the company
20 Net Present Value	21,672.42	Project's value compared with putting the money in the bank
21 Internal Rate of Return	15.4247%	Interest rate that the project is paying

Figure 5.8 - Variation on the financial analysis of an investment project

In a different scenario, assume the sales from year three can go up to $22,000 while keeping all other parameters intact. If you change the sales estimate for years 3 to 10, the result is an NPV of $21,672.42 (positive) and an IRR of 15.4247% (much better than the MARR of 10). This version of the project would be acceptable.

A common practice is to present three scenarios in each proposal: the expected case, the optimistic scenario, and a pessimistic scenario (most likely, best case, and worst case). If the worst-case scenario for this project is that sales in year three rise to $18,000, The expected scenario is sales of $20,000, and the best case is sales of $22,000, holding everything else constant, the results would be as follows:

Table 5.3 - IRR of three possible scenarios of expected sales

Scenario	Expected sales from year three	NPV (MARR=10%)	IRR
Worst case	$18,000	$2,272.69	10.6002%
Most likely	$20,000	$11,972.56	13.0745%
Best case	$22,000	$21,672.42	15.4247%

Since, in this case, all scenarios are favorable, under these conditions, the project would be approved.

In some projects, the worst-case scenario may be adverse, while the expected and optimistic scenario might be favorable. In these cases, it is essential to review the level of risk and the probability of each scenario to determine whether to proceed with the project.

How valid are the results?

Excel is a potent tool, and if a project is not submitting the results needed for approval, it's very tempting to change the profit estimate so that the final result is acceptable. This practice is dangerous because if the initial estimate were honest and well calculated, obtaining the results promised in the modified analysis would be difficult.

Modifying the analyses to measure the effort required to make a project profitable is advisable. For example, if a project shows that sales in year three must be at least $18,000 for the NPV and IRR to be favorable, we must ask ourselves how difficult it is to reach $18,000. If the answer, in all honesty, is that this number is not a problem, then you can present the project to the authorities that analyze it and request the budget to carry it out. If, on the other hand, reaching $18,000 in sales requires an extraordinary effort that has never been achieved before, the project will likely never deliver the results necessary to be considered profitable.

It is much better to identify a potential problem when the project is in the planning and analysis stage than to wait for implementation to realize that the wrong decision has been made.

A good analysis can provide confidence that the project has potential and allow decision-makers to compare different investment alternatives. The IRR and NPV will enable you to compare the expected results of various projects, such as technology, marketing, or production, to name a few. These analyses allow you to decide what is best for the organization's future.

5.9.- Summary

- Money, if invested wisely, yields interest.
- A hundred dollars today differs from a hundred dollars a year from now. If someone pays me a hundred dollars today, I can invest it

(in the bank or my business) and have, within a year, more than the hundred dollars with which I started.

- At today's price, money is known as money at present value. The amount of money you will have at some point in the future is known as future value.
- When calculating the future value of money, it is necessary to know the present amount of money (present value), the interest rate paid per period (interest), and the number of periods that will be considered.

- The formula for calculating future value is:

$$F = P(1 + r)^n$$

- The formula for calculating the present value of an amount of money in a given period is:

$$P = \frac{F}{(1 + r)^n}$$

- The function used in Excel to calculate the future value of a quantity is FV for Future Value. The formula PV calculates the present value.
- The investor typically has a base rate of return against which to compare investment opportunities. This reference rate is called the Minimum Acceptable Rate of Return (MARR). The MARR is a base return that would be obtained for an investment under normal conditions.
- Deciding if an investment is attractive requires bringing all the flows generated by that investment to present value and identifying whether the amount received is equivalent, at current prices, to the amount invested.
- The sum of the present values of all the flows of an investment discounted at a specific interest rate is known as the Net Present Value (NPV).
- To know precisely the interest rate obtained from a project, you must find the interest rate that would make the net present value zero. This value is defined as the Internal Rate of Return (IRR).

73

- As an analysis of a project requires estimates of future flows, a common practice is to present three scenarios in each proposal: the expected, optimistic, and pessimistic.
- A good analysis can provide confidence that the project has potential and allow decision-makers to compare different investment alternatives.

5.10.- Review exercises

Questions

1. Why is it said that money changes in value over time?
2. What is the present value?
3. What does the future value of a certain amount mean?
4. What information do I need to calculate the future value of an investment?
5. What is the formula to estimate the future value of a specific amount?
6. What does the Minimum Acceptable Rate of Return mean?
7. What is MARR used for?
8. What is the net present value of an investment?
9. What can be deducted from a project's internal rate of return?
10. Why is it essential to analyze a project's most likely, optimistic, and pessimistic scenarios?
11. How can I use IRR and NPV to analyze an IT project?

Exercises

1. What is the future value of 100 dollars invested for ten years at an interest rate of 5% annually?
2. Which alternative is more attractive: to receive 110 dollars one year from now or 115 dollars in two years, considering an annual rate of return of 4.5%?
3. An insurance company offers a bond that costs 2,500 dollars and pays, at the end of five years, 3,000 dollars. Is it more convenient to put the money in the bank at an interest rate of 5% per year or to accept the insurance company's proposal?

4. What is the net present value of a 1,000 investment that produces returns of 190 per year for ten years, considering a 15% annual interest rate?
5. What is the interest rate you are paying on a 1,000 investment that produces returns of 190 annually for ten years?
6. A computer project requires an investment of $50,000 in the first year and $30,000 in the second year, yielding a profit of $10,000 in the third year and earnings of $15,000 in years four through ten (when its useful life ends). What is the internal rate of return on that project?

Chapter 6

Qualitative Project Analysis

"Not everything that can be counted counts, and not everything that counts can be counted."

William Bruce Cameron, "Informal Sociology", 1963

6.1.- Learning objectives

- Understand how to prioritize current projects and new developments.
- Identify and classify the projects needed.
- Learn how to define infrastructure projects.
- Understand how to qualify projects with non-quantifiable costs and benefits.
- Learn how to integrate a consolidated list of projects.

6.2.- Elements of an IT plan

The job of an organization's IT area is to help the company achieve its goals. A company's operation generally requires several different information systems. Payroll has to be paid, accounting cannot stop, and production must run uninterrupted. The main priority for the IT area is to keep the current systems functioning.

In addition to keeping the company running, the IT area must develop new projects to support future operations or improve current ones. New projects can be classified into three groups: mandatory projects, such as those that must be done to meet some legal requirement; infrastructure projects, which are projects that leave no value in themselves but are required so that other projects work (examples of these would be communication networks or information security systems); and computer projects that support some strategic initiative of the organization.

Once the projects in which the IT area is going to work have been defined, the next step is to determine the hardware and software required, the necessary data management platforms, and the personnel and budget needed for the operation of the area.

6.3.- Current operation and new developments

As mentioned above, the first responsibility of the IT area is to keep current projects running, followed by new developments to support the organization's plans.

To define which current projects require more attention, they can be categorized in a 2x2 table with two axes: the importance of the project for the company and the project's health (in terms of its operational stability). Those projects that are highly important and have poor health require immediate attention. It is essential that they are updated and do not stop operating. Healthy major projects should only be kept running. Unimportant systems in good health are at the bottom of the care list and can continue to run as long as they do not present a problem. Less critical systems with problems follow in the list. It is crucial to assess whether they should be maintained or eliminated.

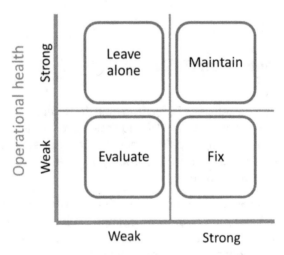

Figure 6.1 - Classification of current projects by importance and stability

6.4.- Necessary projects

Some technology projects can be justified in terms of their costs and benefits. However, some systems must be completed even if their price exceeds the expected tangible benefits. Three kinds of unprofitable projects must be considered in a company's IT plan: those that are required to comply with a legal requirement, infrastructure projects necessary to provide communications or data to other projects, and strategic projects that are necessary to maintain the level of competitiveness of the company or its public image.

The projects necessary to comply with any law or regulation must be included in the IT plan, and their delivery and implementation must be planned within the required times. Examples are systems that protect customer information, report certain activities to government offices, or notify the organization's results to shareholders.

Some necessary projects are those required for compliance with the Sarbanes Oxley Act (SOX), which is mandatory for any company listed on the New York Stock Exchange or operating in the United States. The law seeks to protect investors by improving the quality and accuracy of the financial information issued by the company and demands fines or even jail for non-compliance. Developing the systems to comply with this law is a top priority in any technology plan. Companies like Cemex (NYSE: CX) apply these principles and describe them on their websites [Cemex, 2021].

Minicase - Prioritizing an information security project?

As part of the current information security program, the IT department requires antivirus software on all computers in the company. The procedures also force users to change their passwords from time to time. The measures appear to work; although two competitors fell victim to ransomware attacks, our company has never been attacked. However, the technology area insists that a considerable amount be invested in redundant data systems and copies of our files. Doing that can take resources away from other projects and does not add value to current operations. Should the company analyze this project seriously?

6.5.- Infrastructure projects

Sometimes, it is necessary to carry out specific projects to prepare the way, obtain data, or transport information needed for other projects. These are known as infrastructure projects. An analogy would be like building a road to get to a city. The road itself does not produce any revenue, but having it will allow businesses to operate in different areas.

When an infrastructure project is necessary for a single strategic project, it should be considered part of the cost of the project it serves, and this must be completed just before the project requires it.

On the other hand, if the infrastructure project enables several new initiatives, it should be considered a strategic project and compete for resources with the company's different strategic projects.

Either way, an infrastructure project can wait until just before the first project it serves plans to start operating.

Minicase - A Tale of Two Cities

There are two projects on the to-do list of a business intelligence specialist on a sports team. The first is a system to analyze why 20% of fans with full-season tickets in the box area skip the games. The second is a system to analyze why 10% of the fans in the preferred seats of the stadium chose not to renew their annual subscription this year. How can both projects be prioritized? Which one needs attention first? Why?

6.6.- Non-quantifiable strategic projects

If a project does not produce tangible benefits, the methodology for classifying it is to grade it using a points system according to predefined criteria. [Alanís, 2020]

As an example, in this chapter, the criteria for prioritizing projects are based on four main factors:

- the importance of the program that the project supports,
- how important is the technology's support for the project,
- the availability of the technology and
- what disposition users have.

However, each company is different and can define another group of factors to qualify.

In this case, the First Factor rates the project in general:

The *importance of the program*: It is evident that if, for example, the project to identify new customers is more critical in the organization's plan than the project to eliminate queues at the information desk in a store, then the computer programs for the first would take precedence over those of the second. There is usually a list of priority programs in the company and an order between them. This list can be assigned points. The points given to an overall initiative are the first indicator of where attention should be when planning new projects.

Table 6.1 - General list of projects with scoring.

Project	Importance	Points
A	1	85
B	2	83
C	3	75
D	4	68
E	5	56

The following three factors qualify the computer science role within that project:

The *level of computer support*: There are projects where having a computer is indispensable for its operation. Let's mention, for example, the project to modernize the management of customer credits; this could only be done with the support of computer systems. On the other hand, some projects may not depend so much on technology, for example, the project to improve employees' health by organizing a baseball league. In these cases, although the sports league project may be more critical in some lists of projects, the modernization of the credit management project should receive greater attention from the IT area since that is where the most significant benefit is obtained from the investment.

The *availability of technology*: An essential factor in defining whether a project is done this year, or the following year is whether the technology it requires is available in the organization or the market. If I already have the computer, it may be easier to get the software. On the other hand, technologies are generally more accessible as time goes on. Working with a technology just being developed can be expensive and not yield the expected results. However, projects rejected last year as too costly or complex may be viable this year, given the market changes and new developments.

The fourth factor to consider is the *users' disposition*: Under similar circumstances, it is easier to implement a project for a user who wants it to succeed than for a user who is reluctant to change.

By placing the three factors in a table, you can qualify each project for each element. So, if a project requires full computer support, it receives 10 points in that factor. A project that needs technology that is unavailable or difficult to find could get 3 points in the corresponding line.

Table 6.2 - Projects qualified by value.

Project	Importance of technology	Availability of technology	User's disposition
A	8	10	8
B	10	10	9
C	9	8	8
D	4	3	9
E	8	10	5

The first step in analyzing non-quantifiable projects is assigning a weight to each identified factor. The sum of all elements should be 100. The next step is to calculate, for each project, the percentage value of IT in the program by multiplying the grade obtained by the project on each category times its respective weight. The resulting number is the percentage contribution, which is then multiplied by the program's points on the general plan. A project with a grade of 10 on each item should get 100% of the program's value. A project with 50% on each item should get half of the points available for the program.

Table 6.3 - Projects with the calculation of the value of the contribution of technology in each one

Project	Importance of technology	Availability of technology	User's disposition	IT Value
Weight →	50%	30%	20%	
A	8	10	8	0.86
B	10	10	9	0.98
C	9	8	8	0.85
D	4	3	9	0.47
E	8	10	5	0.80

Combining the percentage of IT contribution for each project (From Table 6.3) with the overall project's points (from Table 6.1) yields a score indicating each project's importance within the year's IT plan.

Table 6.4 - Projects with a score indicating the importance of the technology area.

Project	Importance of technology	Availability of technology	User's disposition	IT Value	Project's initial points	IT points
Weight →	50%	30%	20%			
A	8	10	8	0.86	85	73.1
B	10	10	9	0.98	83	81.3
C	9	8	8	0.85	75	63.8
D	4	3	9	0.47	68	32.0
E	8	10	5	0.80	56	44.8

This calculation allows you to reorder projects differently from the global list. For example, in this case, although Project A has higher priority than Project B, the latter has more points for the IT department, so it deserves more attention.

The resulting list of ordered projects is not final. You have to consider the resources and budget available and decide which project could be completed, starting with the project with the highest score.

Table 6.5 - Projects are ordered according to their importance in the technology area.

Project	IT points
B	81.3
A	73.1
C	63.8
E	44.8
D	32.0

6.7.- Integration of the project plan

The final project plan consists of the projects to keep the current platform running and the new projects, consisting of strategic and infrastructure projects, both quantifiable and non-quantifiable.

The list of projects created with this methodology becomes a tool for negotiation. Considering factors such as the balance of risks (we cannot take only long-term or easy projects), you can start negotiating with the users to define a final IS development plan.

6.8.- Summary

- The first responsibility of the IT area is to keep current projects running, followed by new developments to support the organization's plans.

84

- To define which current projects require more attention, they can be categorized in a 2x2 table with two axes: the importance of the project for the company and the project's health (in terms of its operational stability).
- New projects can be classified in terms of their costs and benefits.
- Three kinds of unprofitable projects must be considered in the work plan: those that are required to comply with a legal requirement, infrastructure projects necessary to provide communications or data to other projects, and strategic projects that are necessary to maintain the level of competitiveness of the company or its public image.
- If the benefits of a project cannot be quantified, the methodology for classifying it is to assign points according to predefined criteria.
- The final project plan consists of the projects to keep the current platform running and the new projects, consisting of strategic and infrastructure projects, both quantifiable and non-quantifiable.
- The list of projects created with this methodology becomes a tool for negotiation. Considering factors such as the balance of risks (we can not take only long-term or easy projects), you can start negotiating with the users to define a final IS development plan.

6.9.- Review questions

Questions
1. Why is it important to focus first on keeping current projects working before considering new developments?
2. What should be done with current projects that are very important but unstable?
3. What should be done with current projects that are unimportant and reasonably stable?
4. How important should the projects required by the government be?
5. How do you decide when to plan an infrastructure project?
6. What criteria can be used to evaluate projects with non-quantifiable benefits?

Exercises
1. Identify two technology infrastructure projects in one company.
2. Identify three required projects in an organization.
3. List two projects with quantifiable benefits and two non-quantifiable ones that operate at a company.

Module III

Developing Business Intelligence Solutions

Chapter 7

Systems Development

"Rushing into manufacturing without being certain of the product is the unrecognized cause of many business failures. People seem to think that the big thing is the factory or the store or the financial backing or the management. The big thing is the product, and any hurry in getting into fabrication before designs are completed is just so much waste time."

Henry Ford, "My Life and Work," 1922

7.1.- Learning objectives

- Describe the systems development life cycle.
- Identify the advantages and disadvantages of prototype development.
- Recognize the advantages and disadvantages of development by end users.
- Understand the levels of automation.
- Identify critical success factors for an information system development project.
- Appreciate the importance of senior management support in projects.
- Appreciate the relevance of continuity of operation.
- List techniques to ensure the continuity of operation of systems in an organization.

7.2.- The systems development life cycle

The components of a business intelligence solution include:

- Computer equipment and software
- Manual procedures
- Models for analysis, planning, control and decision making
- A database

Computer equipment (hardware) can be purchased or rented. Apparently, you just have to pay for it, and that's it. However, the type of equipment to be used, its capacity and requirements must be defined. To define this, you must first specify what you need that hardware to do; That is, what type of programs should be executed.

Getting the software and manual procedures is much more complicated. Computer programs do not appear alone. We have to know what we need them to do, and then buy, build or rent them. The procedures would have to be designed, but they also require training users and ensuring their continuous and problem-free operation for the information system to work.

A technique for creating and implementing an information system is known as the Software Development Life Cycle (SDLC). Figure 7. 1 illustrates the steps of the process [Kendall & Kendall, 2005; Laudon & Laudon, 2019].

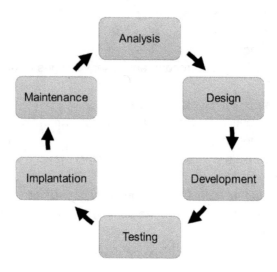

Figure 7.1 – System Development Lifecycle Phases (SDLC)

The phases of the software development life cycle are as follows:

Analysis: Defines what to do

Design: Answers the question of how the system will operate

Development: Ensures that the software specified in the previous two phases is purchased, rented, or built

Testing: Verifies that the system components (people, hardware, and software) perform well together and with the expected workloads.

Implementation: Sets the new system in operation in the organization and manages the change from the old way of doing things to the new.

Maintenance: Ensures that the system continues to operate and provides the required information, correcting errors and reacting to changes in requirements

Each of the identified phases is then broken down.

Analysis

This phase aims to define what the new system should do. Do not worry about how to do it (that's the next phase). Concentrate on the required information, who needs it, and what will be done.

Design

The previous step defined what to do; this phase focuses on who produces the information, how it is processed, what products are generated, and the flow of process data. The question in this phase is: "How is the system going to work?". You must define the components and how they will interact with each other. The design documentation must be detailed enough to build the complete system in the next stage.

Development

The first activity at this stage is to see if a program that works or can be adjusted to our needs is available in the market. If a suitable product exists, it is bought or rented; if it does not, it must be developed. The software must be running error-free before moving on to the next stage.

In some cases, as with enterprise systems (ERP), buying a solution (or part of it) and configuring or adapting it to meet the company's needs is possible.

If the design has sufficient detail, it is possible to send the specifications to external software factories, where programmers develop the requested applications. A software factory can be located anywhere in the world, preferring places where trained personnel are available and willing to work for a lower wage. This practice is known as outsourcing.

Testing

Even if each piece of software works, it is critical to test the entire system, that is, operate the process from where the information originates to where the results are generated. All components (human and mechanical) must work properly and interact without a problem.

It is also essential to test with typical workloads. Sometimes, the software works very well with one or two transactions, but if the operation requires hundreds or thousands of transactions, it is vital to ensure that the system will support real-life environments.

Implementation

The next phase is to put the designed system into operation. The new system represents a change. In most cases, a system replaces an old way of doing things. At this stage, it is essential to train the personnel using the new system and plan to transition from the old one to the new one.

There are three main ways to make the transition: it can be done in one step (one day, the old system is turned off, and the new one is turned on). This option is economical because it requires little expense in the transition but is risky. If the new system does not work or presents problems, this would cause a disaster.

The second way is to run the two systems, the old and the new, in parallel for a while. This option is safe because the old system is only turned off if the new one proves it works. But it is costly as it requires twice as much work for a while.

The third alternative is a phased implementation. If the system can be separated into parts, it is possible to implement a module in one department and then move on with the others. With the first module in place, you can install the next one, and so on, until the complete system is installed.

Maintenance

A computer can break down, or a disk can be damaged, which requires maintenance. But what does it mean to maintain a process or a computer program? Programs always do the same thing; they usually don't modify themselves. Maintenance of software and processes involves two activities: correcting errors not detected in the testing phase; and ensuring that the system complies with providing relevant, complete, and timely information. That is, ensuring that the system is still helpful for making decisions.

Valuable information from yesterday may be less useful today. The problem is that the decisions that a system supports happen in the real world, and the world changes. The system must be modified so that it continues to provide the needed information given the changing conditions of the environment where the decisions it supports exist. Another type of change is when the requirements of the process change, such as when a new tax appears, or interest rates change.

Eventually, conditions change too much, or new opportunities arise, requiring a new information system and a restart of the cycle.

7.3.- Development by prototypes

The systems development lifecycle requires user needs to be identified and defined before moving on to the development stages. This methodology works well for large systems with high levels of complexity, as it helps to divide a problem into parts and identify possible solutions. However, the process takes a lot of time and requires that the issue be well understood before starting the development of solutions.

In the decision-making environment, some decisions that require support come unexpectedly and must be made quickly (which would make it unfeasible to follow a complete development methodology). On the other hand, some problems are so unique that it is difficult to know what it takes to solve them in advance.

If a person wants to buy a suit, the most common solution is to go to a store and try on some models until the person finds the right fit. It is uncommon to go to a store with a list of specifications of what one wants. A similar phenomenon can occur with software. If it's hard for users to know what they need, they may want to try different models until the right solution is found.

The technique used in these cases is called prototyping. Prototype design consists of quickly and inexpensively building an experimental system to evaluate the required functionality [Laudon & Laudon, 2019]. It doesn't have to be a functional system; it can be just a series of images of what would be seen on the screen so the user can feel the proposed functionality.

The process is iterative. The prototype is designed and tested; corrections are made and resubmitted. The process is repeated until an acceptable version is found.

Once the process is complete, if the prototype works, it can be stabilized, documented, and delivered to the end user. The other alternative is to use the prototype as the specification of the desired system, which is then built, tested, and implemented.

7.4.- Development by end users

Some types of systems can be built directly by end users with technologies such as macros in Excel or designing dashboards in Tableau. A positive outcome is that the users easily accept these systems. The problem is that not being built with formal processes, it is typical for systems designed by an end user to have failures, be unable to process large volumes of information or be valid only for a particular person or decision.

A possible danger is that systems designed by end users may not have contingency plans if data is lost. If the company will depend on applications developed by end users, it is convenient to work on using those systems as prototypes and build a formal system based on the design.

An acceptable compromise is establishing specific hardware, software, or data standards for all end-user systems used in the organization. Combining this with awareness of information security and risk prevention processes is essential.

7.5.- Automation or redesign of processes

A new information system brings changes to the organization. Sometimes, the changes are simple. We look for a way to do the same thing that is already done but more efficiently. The technique is called automation.

When automating, it is possible that new bottlenecks are found in the processes or that other problems with the current approaches are discovered. The situation requires a complete review of how things are done, eliminating steps that do not add value and changing others. This approach is called rationalization.

The automation and rationalization of processes make the current approach more efficient. However, there comes the point where the only way to speed up a process further and maximize the potential of the technology is to rethink the activities from the start. This technique is known as business process reengineering. The term was coined by Michael Hammer [Hammer, 1990] and consisted of changing the focus to solve a problem.

Hammer illustrates the idea of reengineering with an analogy. He says that instead of paving dirt roads so you can go faster, it's better to rethink the route and look for better ways to get the expected results. The question is not how I get along the road faster but why I want to get to that destination.

The answer may show that a phone call is enough instead of a new road. Maybe the answer is that we can build a bridge that eliminates much of the trajectory.

The main idea of identifying transformational projects is to change the question. Refocus the effort from how I do this faster to why I do this, or could I do something else? Not all projects require reengineering. These are riskier, time-consuming, face more significant resistance to change, and are more complicated than an automation project. However, in some instances, rethinking processes may be the only solution to a problem in an organization.

7.6.- Critical success factors for a new information system

For a system to be successful, it must work well, but more importantly, it must be used correctly for the people and functions intended.

Building a new information system is a process that requires a lot of effort and the participation of personnel from different areas. If you plan to develop an application to support the sales process, sales personnel must participate in the analysis and design of the solution. This approach requires getting some salespeople out of their sales work to support the creation of a new system.

If the sales managers are not interested in the project and assign their worst salesperson to the task, the resulting system might not work as required. Access to the best salespersons is necessary, distracting them from work for a while, so their ideas can help generate an excellent new solution.

Building a successful application requires the participation of areas that would be the system's users. In turn, they will need senior management's support to accept a drop in productivity (which could result if the best employees are taken out of their jobs for a while to help with the new system).

From the earliest software development projects, it was clear that these projects had special rules [Brooks, 1972]. Top management support and user involvement are critical success factors in developing new information systems.

Among the factors that have proven to be essential for the success of a system's development are:

- Support from senior management
- User engagement
- The professionalism of the development staff
- The proper budget and time
- Clarity in objectives
- Risk management and
- Application of best practices in development

7.7.- The challenges in the continuous operation of an information system

A bank without communications could not verify its customers' account balances to make transactions. A company that could not pay its employees' payroll would face protests or strikes. A brokerage firm that couldn't know whether stock prices were going up or down couldn't survive long. The continuous operation of information systems, especially those critical to the company, is essential.

Operation continuity plans ensure that the company can continue operating despite the technical difficulties it may face. An example would be the state of Colorado's continuity of operations plan, which states that "Continuity of Operations (COOP) is an effort within individual departments and agencies to ensure that their mission essential functions continue to be performed during a wide range of emergencies, including localized weather–related events (tornadoes, floods, blizzards, etc.), long – term power outages, law enforcement activities, acts of terrorism, etc." [Colorado, 2024].

Among the most common challenges for information systems in companies are physical problems. A system could stop operating due to power failures, a water pipe failure that floods the computer center, communications cables outages, or equipment failures. One way to prevent these problems is with backup equipment and redundant systems. If one fails, you can have spare computers ready to work, power systems with emergency batteries, or redundant communication systems. When the operation is critical, some companies have chosen to have two identical systems in different parts of the world. If one were to fail, the other would take control.

A second type of failure is information problems. Data may be accidentally deleted, or storage media may be damaged, making the data impossible to access. A company can protect itself from these problems with periodically updated copies of the information so that, if there is a loss of information, it can use the data from the last backup and lose only a few minutes of work.

The third problem is computer attacks. Computer virus attacks can compromise a system and hackers who seek to access data using social engineering techniques or software such as spyware or Trojan horses. An increasingly common attack is what is known as ransomware, where an attacker encrypts (encodes) a company's data, making it impossible for it to operate, and seeks to charge a ransom for handing over the key to decrypt (decode) the data. Three critical activities to protect the company from computer attacks are installing antivirus and firewall software, having backup copies of the data, and training employees so they don't fall for hackers' tricks.

Minicase – we have an important message for you; just enter your account number and password on this page.

Social engineering consists of trying to trick someone into providing confidential information, such as their username and password. You often see email messages saying that the bank needs you to access information and that you must enter a specific page (providing a link). When you enter that link, they first ask that you register with your username and password. The page is fake; once a victim writes their data, the hacker already has the key to empty their victim's bank accounts or access confidential information. Teaching users how to identify malicious messages and avoid falling into these traps is essential. The moral of the story is that if your bank needs to talk to you, do not click on any link in any message; go directly to the bank's page, call them by phone, or go in person to their offices.

7.8.- Summary

- A technique for creating and implementing an information system is known as the Software Development Life Cycle (SDLC).
- The phases of the software development lifecycle are analysis, design, development, testing, implementation, and maintenance.
- Another technique available is prototyping, where a rapid system that serves as a sample is designed and goes through an iterative

review process. At the end of the process, depending on the type of prototype manufactured, the prototype can be the final product, or it can become the specifications for the formal construction of a complete system.

- End users can develop their applications. It is essential to be careful that these applications follow security protocols to prevent the company from relying on unstable or unsupported systems.
- The support of senior management and users' participation is critical for the success of a new system.
- The continuous operation of information systems, especially those essential for the company's daily operation, is vital.
- Among the most common challenges for information systems in companies are physical problems, problems with information, and computer attacks.

7.9.- Review exercises

Questions

1. What is the systems development lifecycle?
2. What are the steps in the systems development lifecycle?
3. What stage of the life cycle describes what the new system will do?
4. What is the difference between automating and reengineering?
5. What is the product of the design phase of a system?
6. What is tested during the testing stage of a system?
7. What are the three ways to implement a system, and what are the advantages and disadvantages of each one?
8. Why is it essential to give maintenance to a system?
9. What is a prototype design, and when is it convenient to use?
10. What advantages and problems can end-user application development present?
11. Why is it critical to have the support of senior management when carrying out an information technology project?
12. What is a mission essential function?
13. Why are continuity plans necessary?

Exercises

1. Interview the technology manager at a company, ask them to remember a successful project, and ask if any of the critical factors mentioned in this chapter occurred.
2. Interview the technology manager at a company and ask if they remember a project that has failed and what caused the failure.

3. Describe a business process reengineering project.
4. Identify and describe an automation project.
5. Find an e-mail message that uses social engineering techniques to attempt an attack on the receiver.

Chapter 8

Project Management & Risk Management Tools

055:55:20 Swigert: ...we've had a problem here. [Pause.]

055:55:28 Lousma: This is Houston. Say again, please.

055:55:35 Lovell: [Garble.] Ah, Houston, we've had a problem. We've had a Main B Bus Undervolt."

Astronauts aboard Apollo XIII reporting an incident to Mission Control Center at NASA, April 1970, [Woods et al., 2017].

8.1.- Learning objectives

- Identify the main challenges of IT Project Management.
- Learn about project management tools.
- Understanding the Advantages and Limitations of a Gantt Chart.
- Know how to use a PERT chart.
- Be able to apply the concept of critical path to project management.
- Understand the concept of risk management.

8.2.- Project management tools

History is full of great projects: the pyramids of Egypt, the Roman Colosseum, Napoleon's great battles, and the conquest of New Spain, to name a few. We know that in every large project, one or more coordinators oversee planning and execution. Although we have yet to learn the details of the management tools used in large historical projects, there has been enough experience to know that certain activities, tools, and functions promote a successful project.

The first important point is to define a project. A project is a series of activities aimed at achieving a goal. Every project has a start and an endpoint. If the activities do not have a point of completion, then we are no longer talking about a project but a job; in those cases, different management principles apply.

If a project is too large to handle, it is best to divide it into activities or sub-projects. These, in turn, can be subdivided into more specific activities until you reach a point where each activity is manageable.

A project manager's job is to ensure that each activity is resourced and completed in time to deliver the finished project by the agreed date.

Any software development job is a project and must be managed. It is essential to define a starting and end point, define the sub-components, and allocate resources and assignees to each one.

The two most used tools to help a leader manage the complexities of a project are Gantt charts and PERT charts. Gantt charts list a project's activities and their start and end dates in a horizontal bar chart. This tool can graphically represent the times of each activity and the resources needed at each stage. PERT (Program Evaluation and Review Technique) charts show activities and their dependencies, helping to identify areas of opportunity and activities that should be given particular attention because they are part of the "critical path," which are a series of activities that, if delayed, would cause a change in the final delivery date of the project.

8.3.- Gantt charts

The most well-known tool for managing projects is the Gantt chart. Gantt charts are a very visual way to analyze the stages of a project and see its status. The graph consists of a two-dimensional model where the horizontal axis represents time, and the vertical axis lists the names of the activities that make up the project. Each activity is drawn as a horizontal bar; its start point coincides with the start date of that activity, and its length matches its duration, so its endpoint marks the expected end date. Table 8.1 lists activities in a project, their expected duration, and the activities that must be completed before they start (dependencies). The Gantt chart of Figure 8.1 is based on the table's information.

Table 8.1 - List of a project's activities, duration and dependencies.

Activity	Requires	Duration
A	Nothing	2
B	A	3
C	B	2
D	C	1
E	B	1
F	E	3
G	Nothing	3
H	G	3
I	H	1

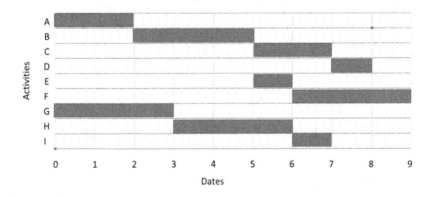

Figure 8.1 – Gantt chart.

What can be interpreted from Figure 8.1 is that there are nine activities identified in the project, named A through H. Activity A and Activity G can start right when the project begins. The last activity before completing the project is activity F. If everything works as planned, the project will take nine days to finish.

The graph also indicates that some activities can co-occur, for example, A, G, and part of B. Therefore, if each activity requires a dedicated team, the project will need at least three different teams.

If completed processes are colored green at completion, processes that have already started are colored blue. If we were on day 4, for example, the graph would show us, at a glance, if everything is on time or something is delayed or ahead of schedule.

Minicase - A Tool from Another Century

In 1896, a Polish engineer who managed a steel mill south of Polynya became interested in ideas and techniques for managing projects that allowed for the visualization of activities and times. His ideas were published in 1931 in Polish and Russian, two languages little known in the West. By then, Henry Gantt had already published and popularized a similar method in 1910 and 1915. Today, these types of charts are known as Gantt charts. Originally, graphs were used to identify employee productivity levels and see who was more or less productive. The story's moral: it's not enough to invent something. It's also essential to make it known. [Gantt.com, 2024]

8.4.- PERT diagrams

Although Gantt charts show activities over time, they do not illustrate the dependency between activities nor what would happen if a particular activity was delayed. Another tool used in project management that helps identify dependencies is PERT diagrams, an abbreviation for Program Evaluation and Review Technique. This type of graph illustrates activities in the form of nodes and the sequence of nodes as arrows connecting one to the next. The diagram helps understand which activities must be completed before other activities can start and which are independent of previous processes. For example, you can only put the roof on a house if you have built the walls. The tool also identifies the critical path, i.e., the longest chain of activities. If any element of the chain is delayed, this would have a direct effect on the project's expected completion date.

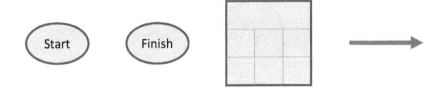

Figure 8.2 – Elements of a PERT chart

Four symbols make up a PERT diagram: start point, endpoint, node or activity, and arrow. The steps to create a PERT chart are:

1. Create the project's node network.
2. In each node, write the name of the activity and its duration.
3. Calculate each node's early start and finish time, starting with those that connect to the start point (with a start time of zero) (this activity fills the top row of every node).
4. The project's end time is the latest end time of those nodes connecting directly to the endpoint.
5. Calculate the late finish and start for each node, starting with the nodes that connect to the endpoint using the project's end time as the latest finish time.
6. Calculate the slack time for each node.
7. Identify the critical path (nodes that have zero slack).

Activity Name		
Early Start	Duration	Early Finish
Late Start	Slack	Late Finish

Figure 8.3 - Content of an activity node in a PERT chart.

An activity node is represented as a rectangle and includes the name of the activity at the top. The following line consists of the earliest start, duration, and end times. The bottom line lists the latest start time, the slack, and the latest finish time.

To create the project's node network:

1. Place the starting point.
2. Identify what activities can start right when the project starts (that depend on no other activity) and connect them to the start point.
3. Identify which activities follow the activities you just placed, put them on the graph, and connect them.
4. Connect the last activity(s) (those with no following activities) to the endpoint.

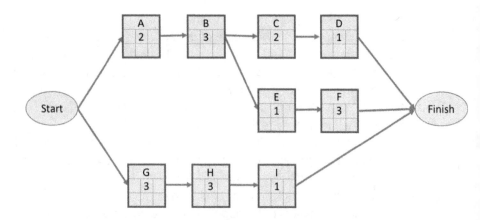

Figure 8.4 – PERT chart's node network from table 8.1

To calculate the earliest start and end time:

The earliest start time for nodes that depend on the start point is zero. The termination point of those nodes is the sum of the early start time plus the expected duration of the activity. The early start time of a node is equal to the early termination time of the node that precedes it. If two nodes are needed to start a third, the earliest start time of the resulting node will be the termination time of the preceding node that terminates later. The duration time of a project will be the later termination time of the node that connects to the endpoint.

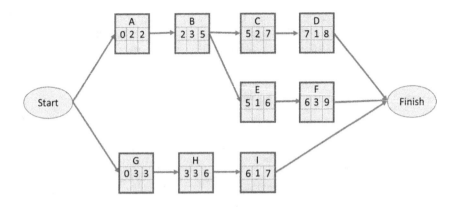

Figure 8.5 – PERT chart with early start and finish times from table 8.1.

The project duration time (the latest termination time of the nodes connecting to the endpoint) becomes the late end time of any node that attaches directly to the endpoint. The late start time for each node is the subtraction of the late end time minus the duration of the activity. If two nodes follow the same previous node, the latest termination time of the last node would be the lowest late start time of any of the nodes that follow it (if a node terminates later, even if feasible for some of its successors, the node with the earliest time would no longer start on time). Calculate the slack of each node by subtracting the early start point from the late start point.

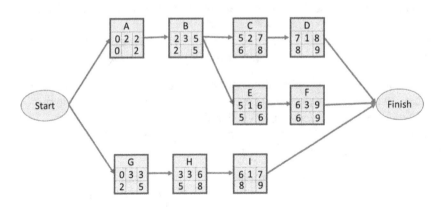

Figure 8.6 – PERT chart with late start and finish times

Some nodes may have more slack than others. The slack does not mean that every node could be delayed by that much. If a node is delayed, its successors' start and finish times change, so the time and slack of the entire project must be recalculated. However, some nodes have a slack value of zero. Those activities must be completed on time. Losing a day in any of those activities would delay the final delivery of the project by the same amount. Nodes that have zero slack are known as the critical path.

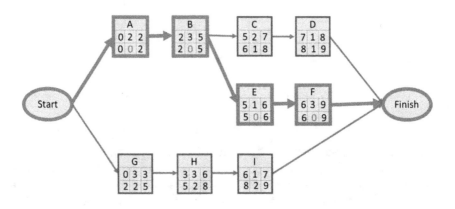

Figure 8.7 - Critical path on a PERT chart

From Figure 8.7, it can be deduced that the longest route is occupied by activities A, B, E, and F, with a total duration of 9 days, so if everything works as it should, the project will conclude in 9 days. If there was a problem with any of those activities, let's say activity E was delayed by one day, then the final project due date would now be delayed by one day.

On the other hand, the path that connects nodes A, B, C, and D is non-critical, meaning that if process C were to be delayed by one day, the project could still be completed in 9 days. Similarly, if any activities on the path connecting nodes G, H, and I were delayed by one or even two days, the delivery date would not be affected.

Knowing the slack times of processes is vital in case there are limited resources. They help the project manager decide which process should receive the resources and which can wait.

Let's assume that activities I and F are active simultaneously, and both require a computer, but only one is available; the second computer arrives tomorrow. The administrator must assign the computer equipment to activity F (because that activity is critical and cannot be delayed). This decision would cause a one-day delay in activity I, but that process can tolerate that delay without affecting the project's final delivery date. These charts help in some of a project manager's most difficult decisions.

Minicase - That computer was for me.

One of the benefits of PERT charts is that they help the project manager make difficult decisions about resource allocation. Imagine a project with two activities simultaneously: Act 1 and Act 2. Both activities require a computer. However, only one computer is available; the second one will arrive tomorrow. If the project's PERT charts showed that Act 1 is part of the critical path and Act 2 has at least one day's slack, a good project manager would assign the available computer to Act 1, regardless of who the original recipient was. The person in charge of Act 2 is going to claim his equipment. It will explain that the process will be delayed, and that the responsibility should fall on the project manager. The project manager can say that it is an executive decision made for the good of the overall project. Act 2 can wait a day without affecting the project's final outcome, while Act 1 can't be stopped.

8.5.- Risk management

All security measures cost money or time. An extra computer, some disks to back up information, or even employee training courses all require valuable resources. In deciding how much to spend on protection and how to use the company's resources, it is necessary to do a risk and cost analysis.

Risk management consists of three steps:

1. Risk Identification
2. Risk Analysis
3. Risk Control

Risk Identification
Step one lists everything that can pose risks to the company, its products, or its projects. Among the risks to be analyzed would be risks of technology, people, organization, requirements, or cost estimation.

Risk Analysis
The next phase is to analyze the likelihood that one of those identified risks will occur and the effect that risk may have on the organization. The analysis requires mapping to a quadrant where one axis is the probability of finding the risk (high, medium, or low), and the other is the effect that the company might encounter if the risk were to materialize (high, medium, or low). Figure 8.8 illustrates a table of risk exposure analysis.

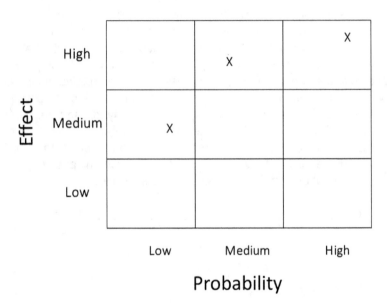

Figure 8.8 -Risk analysis table

Risk Control
Once the risks are qualified, it becomes clear that some are more critical than others. For example, something highly likely, which, when it happens, will have a catastrophic effect on the company, is something that the company must take care of and seek to eliminate, or at least prepare for, while something unlikely and with a low effect, it is perhaps an acceptable risk that will be dealt with when it occurs.

High-probability risks with medium or high effect and high-effect risks with medium or high probabilities are unacceptable. There are two ways to treat them: to reduce the likelihood (by investing in backup equipment, for example) and to mitigate the effect (by investing in copies of information or emergency procedures).

Risks with low probability and low effect may be acceptable and can be dealt with by the company if they occur.

Medium risks require preparation should they occur (planning what to do if they appear). But do not require investing in equipment or materials.

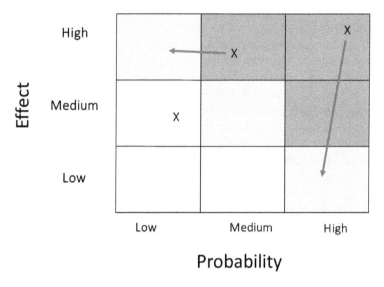

Figure 8.9 - Risk mitigation and acceptance zones.

8.6.- Integration of risk management data into a project budget

For a consultant to charge a fixed price for a project requires knowing or having a reasonable estimate of all of its costs. Any miscalculated cost would eventually have to be covered by the consultant. If the quoted price is fixed, the non-estimated costs would have to come from the expected profits. A project with enough miscalculations can become unprofitable.

Initially, the price of a project is the result of calculating its costs and adding the expected profit to it. For example, if a project requires resources and personnel that cost 80, and you want to make a profit of 40, the final price should be 120, which would be the price if the project had no risk.

111

All risks must be identified and qualified to estimate the cost that the risk would add to the project. If there is any risk with high cost and high probability, the project will likely fail, so a quote should not be offered to the client. However, if it is possible to mitigate high risks with effect or probability mitigation measures, the cost of mitigation measures should be added to the project cost. An example would be to buy an uninterrupted power supply to mitigate the effect of a power failure.

Assuming that, in our project, with a price of 120, 15 had to be invested for mitigation measures, the cost would now be 135.

Once mitigation costs are integrated, some risks are likely to remain at medium and low levels. While these risks generally don't jeopardize the project, they come at a cost. The cost of a one-day delay or repairing a piece of equipment must be considered on the project. The way to quote is, based on the level and number of minor faults identified, a percentage of the price can be reserved as a form of accident insurance. The project would be safe if any of that fund needs to be used. If money from this insurance is left over at the end, the surplus accumulates in an account for other projects that might exceed your estimates. This amount to be added to the final price is the contingency cost. Assuming a contingency cost of 10% is estimated, then the project would now cost 148.5, and that would be the price to quote for the project. A lower price would run the risk of leaving the project without profits. Figure 8.10 shows the elements of integrating risk calculation into a project's price.

Cost of time and materials	80
Expected profit	+ 40
Sub-total price	120
Mitigation costs	+ 15
Sub-total price	135
Contingency cost	+ 13.5
Final Price	147.5

Figure 8.10 – Factoring risk into a project's final price

8.7.- Summary

- The development effort of a new information system should be viewed as a project and can be managed using project management tools.
- Among the most common tools for managing projects are Gantt charts and PERT charts
- Risk management helps decide how much to spend on protection, and what to use the company's resources. It consists of three steps: risk identification, analysis, and control.

8.8.- Review exercises

Questions

1. What is the difference between a Gantt chart and a PERT chart?
2. How can you prevent possible data loss if a hard drive is damaged?
3. What kind of businesses would require redundant (double) data processing facilities?
4. What are the steps in the risk management process?

Exercises

1. You are responsible for organizing a benefit concert for a well-known band. On the day of the concert, several activities are needed:

Activity	Requires	Duration
A.- Open the concert hall	Nothing	1 hour
B.- Install the sound	A	3 hours
C.- Install the decorations	A	4 hours
D.- Meet the band at the airport	Nothing	1 hour
E.- Bring the band to the concert hall	D	1 hour
F.- Do a sound checks	B & E	2 hours
G.-Start the concert	C & F	3 hours

- Prepare a Gantt chart of the activities to be carried out.
- Prepare a PERT chart of the activities to be carried out.

- If the concert ends at 11 p.m., when is the latest the hall can open?
- What time is the latest you could pick up the band at the airport?
- What would be the critical path on the day of the concert?

2. Visit a bank and look at what's in the lobby before the cashiers.
- Identify a risk that exists and that the bank has sought to reduce.
- If a risk is that the building could catch fire and cause the death of people, what measures could be taken to reduce the likelihood of a fire? How could the possibility of fatalities be reduced?
- Identify a risk that exists and that the bank has decided to accept (that it does not have measures in place to eliminate or reduce its effects).

Chapter 9

Technology Infrastructure

"But if these machines were ingenious, what shall we think of the calculating machine of Mr. Babbage? What shall we think of an engine of wood and metal which can not only compute astronomical and navigation tables to any given extent, but render the exactitude of its operations mathematically certain through its power of correcting its possible errors? What shall we think of a machine which can not only accomplish all this, but actually print off its elaborate results, when obtained, without the slightest intervention of the intellect of man?"

Edgar Allan Poe, Maelzel's Chess-Player, 1836.

9.1.- Learning objectives

- Identify the components of a technology platform.
- Describe the parts and operation of the hardware platform.
- Describe the functions of an operating system.
- Explain how application software operates.
- Understand the three key technologies that support the Internet.
- Describe the advantages and disadvantages of cloud computing.

9.2.- Components of a technology infrastructure

Technology infrastructure, the platform necessary for a business intelligence application to operate, refers to much more than just a computer.

A computer (hardware) alone is useless. It needs a series of programs with instructions on interpreting keystrokes, moving information to and from memory, and displaying results on a screen (to name a few). Those instructions show the computer how to operate and are the operating system.

Solving real problems (such as Business Intelligence) requires specialized application programs that run on the operating system. They include the procedures and calculations needed to convert data into useful information.

Data might come from more than one place. Sometimes, it is stored on different computers. Therefore, application programs also need communication between computers, sometimes through the Internet.

Technology infrastructure refers to the hardware, operating systems, applications, and communication programs that turn data into useful information. Figure 9.1 shows an outline of the components of a technology platform.

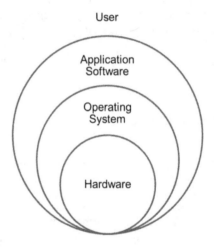

Figure 9.1 – Components of a technology platform

9.3.- Hardware platforms

Hardware is the computer equipment where information is processed. A computer has several components: input and output equipment, processing units, memory, and secondary storage. Figure 9. 2 shows a general outline of a computer.

Input units enter information into the computer. The most common examples are a keyboard, mouse, camera, and microphone. Some computers may also have touch-sensitive screens or fingerprint readers.

Other input equipment might be scanners, barcode readers, or magnetic stripe readers.

Output units are how we get information out of the computer. The most common output units are displays and printers. Other typical output units are the speakers with which the computer can send signals (beeps) or even play some audio. More specialized output units can be robots with movement or vibrators (to indicate on a handheld device that the information has been received).

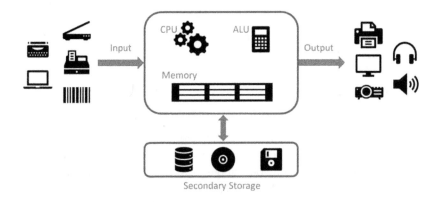

Figure 9.2 - General layout of a computer

Inside the processing unit are three main components: The Central Processing Unit or CPU, the arithmetic logic unit or ALU, and the main memory. The CPU is the part that controls the movement of information among components, instructs the ALU to perform some operation, or tells the memory where to store a value. The ALU performs mathematical functions or comparisons between two numbers the CPU provides, returning the result. Main memory is where the data and programs running on the computer are stored.

A computer program is a series of instructions stored in the computer's memory. The CPU takes the first instruction and executes it, then moves on to the next until the program ends.

Since, in many computers, the main memory requires power to operate, sometimes it is necessary to store data outside the computer on secondary storage units such as disks, tapes, or USB sticks (to avoid having to reenter the programs every time the computer is powered on). When activated, most computers have instructions for downloading the operating system programs from secondary storage to main memory so that they can start operations.

Physical size, processing speed, and memory capacity are essential to define the speed of a computer. Electricity must travel from one component of the computer to the next. Smaller computers take less time to move data around. Memory is crucial because moving information within memory is faster than bringing it from external devices. A machine with limited memory must wait to bring in data from secondary storage drives to keep operating.

The top microcomputer manufacturers are Dell, HP, Apple, Acer, and Lenovo. IBM, Hitachi, and Unisys manufacture more powerful mainframe computers for large enterprises or complex operations.

9.4.- Operating systems

As explained earlier, hardware alone is useless. It needs programming to be able to send something to print or display it on the screen. Those instructions are called the operating system. There are some standard operating systems designed for different computer hardware. To print something, you have to give the order to the operating system, which will send the correct commands for the hardware.

The most common PC operating systems are Windows and Mac OS X. Other operating systems, such as Unix or Linux, run on medium and large computers. Small devices like phones or tablets generally use Android, iOS, Windows Phone OS, or Symbian.

The advantage of standard operating systems is that if a program runs on Windows, nothing needs to be changed if the operating system runs on a Dell computer or an HP machine.

9.5.- Application software

Application software runs on top of the operating system. These are the computer programs that process information. Examples include business applications such as SAP, ORACLE, or Microsoft Dynamics; tailor-made systems such as payroll or inventory; database platforms; and packages such as Word, Excel, or Tableau.

The user works with the application software and usually does not have to worry if they change the computer or even the operating system.

9.6.- Internet

A computer can work with the information in its main memory and what it can access from its secondary storage. Sometimes, it is necessary to bring data from other computers in the same office or the other side of the world. The data comes via computer networks, connections between computers that allow them to exchange information. The most prevalent network today is the Internet.

The Internet is a communications architecture that allows different computer networks worldwide to interact with each other. The Internet emerged in the United States in the 1970s but became popular in the mid-1990s. By 2020, more than half of the earth's population had access to the Internet [Kahn & Dennis, 2022].

The Internet is based on three key technologies [Laudon & Traver, 2018]:

- Packet switching
- TCP/IP Communications Protocol
- Client-server communications architecture.

Packet switching is a method of dividing messages into smaller units called packets. Each packet includes identifying information that describes the type of information it contains, what part of the message it is, where it comes from, and its destination.

Each packet may follow a different route. The packages are reassembled upon arrival at the destination, and the original message is recomposed on the receiving computer.

Figure 9.3 shows how packet switching consists of each node sending each packet to the next computer on the network toward the recipient's address. In turn, the computer receiving the message forwards it to the next available computer in the right direction until the packet reaches its destination. If a route is busy or a node is not responding, the message is sent by an alternate route. Eventually, all packages arrive at the destination computer; the target computer acknowledges the packet's arrival and reassembles the entire message from its parts. If the source computer doesn't get a receipt stating that all the packages arrived correctly, it simply sends a replacement package.

Figure 9.3 illustrates the military origins of the Internet network. If a node were turned off for any reason, the network would not stop working because there are many ways to get the information to its destination. Therefore, when there is a problem or natural disaster in a city, and it cannot transmit data, the network does not stop. The messages that naturally follow that path use another route without requiring users or administrators to do anything special.

However, this advantage has also become a problem. Just as a natural disaster cannot stop the Internet, neither can a decree of some government institution. Users usually find ways to circumvent any barrier that is placed. There are documented cases of popular revolts, coordinated from the Internet, that governments cannot easily control. One example occurred in the spring of 2011 when protests in different Arab countries culminated in overthrowing several local governments. The event is known as the Arab Spring [History, 2020].

Fake news is another problem exacerbated by the Internet. Since there is no central authority, it is almost impossible to delete a message, even if it contains intentionally erroneous information. In the same way, if someone uploads an offensive photograph, it is nearly impossible to remove it from the network.

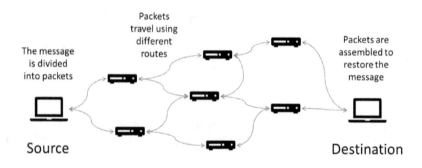

Figure 9.3 – Packet switching

The second key element that supports the Internet is the TCP/IP (Transmission Control Protocol/Internet Protocol) communications protocol. This standard establishes the packet addressing scheme, the way sending and receiving computers are connected, and the way the message is separated into packets on the sending computer and the packets are reassembled on the receiving computer.

The third element, the client-server communications architecture, is a computing model where one computer (the client) connects with another (the server) to ask for information, minimizing the amount of data transmitted using communication networks. The data processing happens on the server. The only information that travels through the web is the client's request and the page with the response. In this way, there is no need to send the complete contents of a database to answer a client's request, making communications faster.

For example, if you enter the Google page and type "business intelligence," Google will respond with a message stating that there are about 2.3 billion results, followed by the first ten results of its list. What has happened is that the request traveled to Google's computers. Google's server searched their data and responded by sending only the first names in its list. This information can be sent quickly to the client's computer because only one phrase travels one way, and a page travels back through the network. The rest of the almost 80 million responses are only sent if they are requested. The user can request page two or three, and Google will respond with them.

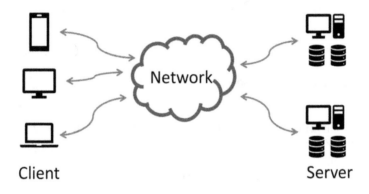

Figure 9.4 – Client-server architecture

The client-server communications architecture results in the network responding quickly and can be used with any client computer, even if these are not necessarily very powerful. That allows personal computers, tablets, phones, and even kitchen appliances to interact with the network without requiring expensive processors, a lot of memory, or large storage capacity.

Many other protocols and programs support the Internet, such as HTTP, SMTP, and FTP protocols, as well as software applications.

Minicase - "Fake news" and its political influence.

False news reports that appear with the emergence of social networks, also known as "fake news," consist of stories that seem to be accurate reports but have no support or reliable sources.

Fake news creates "competing versions of information and the truth" designed and broadcast to deceive or manipulate people for economic or political gain. However, the term has also been used to discredit accurate news or contrary opinions.

The challenge of fake news is discussed in an interview published by the United Nations [Dickinson, 2018]. You can find the full interview here: https://news.un.org/en/audio/2018/05/1008682

9.7.- Cloud computing

An example of client-server architecture mentioned in the previous section is what is known as cloud computing, where computing and storage power resides in large data servers. The user can access these from almost anywhere without needing sophisticated devices as a client.

The advantage of cloud computing is that it can serve users almost immediately. Once an application is placed in the cloud, adding a new location to the system requires only connecting the new office to the Internet. Once connected, everyone in the office can access the full power of the application without investing in expensive equipment or modifying facilities. Another advantage when applications are shared among many users is that the cost of creating and operating cloud solutions is distributed among many participants, making it quite economical.

One disadvantage of cloud solutions is that the operation depends on a data connection. If the link were to fail, there would be no access to any information. Another disadvantage cited by some users is that data that may be confidential is moved on public networks, so it is vital to measure the security levels of these applications before committing to use them.

Minicase – Salesforce, a complete CRM system installed in 15 minutes.

Salesforce.com, Inc. is a San Francisco-based company that builds and operates a cloud CRM platform. Customers can hire their services and run a complete CRM solution for their company, paying only a monthly rent for each user they want to access the platform.

A complete CRM solution for a medium to small business could cost tens of thousands of dollars and require a year to implement. Using Salesforce takes little time to boot, requires no additional hardware to a PC and an Internet connection, and could cost between $50 and $200 per month, depending on the number of people that need to access the information. You can watch videos explaining how the platform works on the company's web page on Salesforce.com

9.8.- Summary

- Technology infrastructure refers to the hardware, operating systems, applications, and communication programs that turn data into useful information.
- Hardware alone is useless. It needs programming to be able to send something to print or display it on the screen. Those instructions are called the operating system.
- Application software runs on top of the operating system. These are the computer programs that process information.
- The Internet is a communications architecture that allows different computer networks worldwide to interact with each other.
- Internet is based on three key technologies: packet switching, TCP/IP communications protocol, and client-server communications architecture.
- Cloud computing is a variant of the client-server model where computing and storage power resides in large data servers. The user can access these from almost anywhere without needing sophisticated devices as a client.

9.9.- Review exercises

Questions

1. What are the components of a technology architecture?
2. What is hardware?
3. What are the main parts of a computer?
4. What does an operating system do?
5. Mention some examples of operating systems.
6. Mention some examples of software applications.
7. What are the three key technologies of the Internet?
8. What are the advantages of cloud computing?
9. What are the disadvantages of cloud computing?

Exercises

1. Identify the input units of a computer.
2. List at least five output units of a computer.
3. Find four hardware vendors.
4. Identify two different brands of computers that use the same operating system.
5. Find information about cloud-based ERP solution providers.

Module IV

The Information Technology Industry

Chapter 10

Technology Provider Management

"Hence the skillful fighter puts himself into a position which makes defeat impossible and does not miss the moment for defeating the enemy.

Thus, it is that in war the victorious strategist only seeks battle after the victory has been won, whereas he who is destined to defeat first fights and afterwards looks for victory."

Sun Tsu, "The Art of War" Chapter IV, Fifth Century BC.

10.1.- Learning objectives

- Identify the phases of the procurement process.
- Define the activities that occur during the need recognition phase.
- Explain how a contract is formalized.
- Understand how a public bidding process works.
- Identify the responsibilities of the parties during the execution of a contract.
- Recognize the importance and process of change control.
- Identify a technological partner's roles in defining, developing, and operating projects.
- Appreciate the value of treating colleagues with respect and honesty.

10.2.- The phases of the technology purchase process

The amount organizations spend on computer applications and information technology purchases is a significant part of the company's total operating budget. At the same time, the computer equipment and solutions market can be highly lucrative for specialized organizations. Understanding the technology purchase process is critical for sellers and buyers.

Many believe that a purchase starts when a buyer sends a request for proposal (RFP) to potential suppliers; however, the process begins much earlier. The specifications of the solutions to buy start with identifying a business need. The complete procurement process consists of three stages [Alanís, 2020]:

- Recognition of the need
- Formalization of the contract
- Contract Administration

The first phase, recognition of the need, starts with identifying and defining the company's needs. Designing a good solution requires an understanding of existing and emerging technologies. Preparing a detailed RFP to attract possible suppliers at reasonable prices involves experience.

The second phase, the contract's formalization, is generally a very rigid process handled by areas specialized in negotiation or acquisitions. Depending on the investment required and the company's policies, the purchase can be awarded directly to a specific supplier, require two or more quotes from different suppliers, or even need a public bidding process. Public bidding is a ceremony widely used in government organizations, where suppliers deliver their offers in a sealed envelope. All bids are publicly opened and analyzed to select a winner.

Once a winner has been chosen, the contract is formalized and executed. During the execution phase, the project is developed. It is essential to be careful with change control and note that looking for contract extensions without additional bidding is possible.

10.3.- Recognition of the need

A project can be triggered at the initiative of a user or by the technology area. In any case, users must be involved in defining needs and exploring possible solutions.

The recognition of the need corresponds to the analysis and design phases of the project in the Systems Development Lifecycle methodology (SDLC) described above. At this stage, exploring alternatives, analyzing the market, and testing different solutions is essential before committing to a final design.

In many cases, recognizing the need is only an initial diagnosis to justify allocating resources to analyze and design a solution. Either way, an estimate of the size of the problem (expected costs and benefits) is required to align the project against other projects competing for resources at this stage.

10.4.- Formalization of the contract

Once there is an understanding of the need, be it a custom development, a package, or a cloud application, the next step is to contact suppliers to measure their capabilities and receive their offers.

One way to initiate contact with a vendor is by issuing a Request for Proposal (RFP). This document can be as simple as a phone call or an email indicating the type of solution being sought. The RFP can be targeted to a specific company or open to the entire market. The supplier assigns a business leader who interviews the participants to prepare the requested proposal.

During this initial phase, the buyer can refine the requirements and better understand the supplier's capabilities. It is possible to work on the same project with more than one supplier as long as everyone understands that they are working with several companies and that there is only a final decision or commitment from either party once a contract is signed. Requesting a non-disclosure agreement (NDA) to protect privileged information shared at this stage is common.

The actual purchase is usually carried out by an area specialized in negotiation and acquisitions, generally known as the purchasing department. Depending on the amount, the purchasing department can acquire the defined solution with the recommended supplier or ask for more quotes from different vendors. They usually seek to demonstrate that the selected supplier is the most convenient for the company.

Governments and public entities have a set of laws governing the procurement process. In the United States, most federal government procurement is governed by the Federal Acquisition Regulations. In Canada, contracts are governed by the Government Contracts Regulations, which aim to ensure that government agencies in Canada "get the best value for Canadians while improving access, competition, and equity" [Government of Canada, 2024].

In Mexico, government purchases are the subject of the country's Political Constitution, which in its article 134 states:

"The acquisitions, leases, and disposals of all types of goods, provision of services of any nature, and the contracting of works carried out shall be awarded or carried out through public bidding. Solvent proposals may be freely presented in a sealed envelope, which shall be opened publicly, to assure the State of the best available conditions regarding price, quality, financing, timeliness, and other relevant circumstances."

H. Congreso de la Unión, "Constitución Política de los Estados Unidos Mexicanos", Art. 134

Article 134 is operationalized at the federal level in the Law on Acquisitions, Leases, and Services of the Public Sector [Cámara de Diputados del H. Congreso de la Unión, 2014]. Different agencies in different states and countries have individual laws, but the processes are similar in scope and purpose. Figure 10.1 shows the general steps for bidding on a government contract.

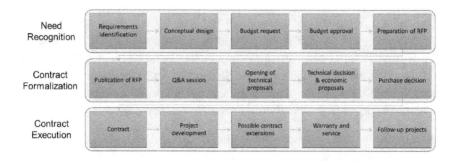

Figure 10.1 - Steps for a government purchase process by public bidding

Minicase - who provides a better service?

For most people, taking a car to a mechanic is stressful. There are some excellent shops, but there are also some horror stories. The following are two similar stories with very different endings:

User one takes the car with a mechanic on Wednesday. The workshop asks the user to leave the vehicle for inspection and call in the afternoon for a quote. The workshop had no information when the customer called in the afternoon but told the user they would have a quote the following morning. The client finally received a quote for the work on Thursday at noon and approved it. The shop promises the car will be ready on Saturday morning, but the car is finally out by Tuesday.

In case two, the user takes the car to the mechanic on Wednesday. The workshop asks the user to leave the vehicle for inspection and promises a quote by the afternoon of the following day. At noon on Thursday, the customer receives the work proposal that indicates that the shop has to order some missing parts, which will arrive on Monday, be installed on Tuesday, and that the car should be ready the following Wednesday. On Tuesday, the user gets a message that the vehicle is ready for pickup (one day earlier than promised).

Both workshops took the same time. Who gave a better service?

10.5.- Execution of the contract

Once a supplier is selected and a contract signed, control of the project returns to the development area handling the project. It is essential to understand the scope of the agreement. The supplier commits to specific delivery dates, and the customer commits to provide certain facilities and equipment to expedite the work.

The customer is responsible for ensuring that the received product complies with the requested specifications and is complete with the manuals and training agreed to in the contract.

The purchasing area must receive periodic progress reports to process any partial payment agreed upon in the contract.

During the execution of a contract, it is possible to find new areas of opportunity or require changes to the original design. It is essential to evaluate these modifications as they can affect the cost or delivery time of the final project. The way to handle changes is with a change control procedure where:

1. The area identifying the opportunity fills out a form describing the requested change.
2. The project manager evaluates the appropriateness of forwarding the request to the supplier.
3. The supplier analyzes the modification request and decides if it can be examined or rejected.
4. The supplier examines the requested change and identifies its effect on price and delivery dates.
5. The supplier writes a change proposal (with costs and times) and delivers it to the project manager.
6. The project manager and purchasing area analyze and approve or reject the change proposal.

10.6.- Delivery of the project

A project is only complete once it is available to the user, and it does not require anyone from the vendor or the technology area to modify the software or tell the user what to do. There are two parts to declaring a project complete: It must run with no errors, and the user has to know how to operate it.

Eliminating errors requires testing. All the solution components must work well independently, but they must also work well together.

User training and data migration are also critical steps before releasing a project. The best software project is complete only if the user knows how to operate it.

Once the supplier has complied with everything stipulated in the contract, the project manager writes and signs a letter of acceptance. A copy of the letter goes to the purchasing department so they can process the final payments and close the contracts. At this time, the warranty period begins to run, and the company can sign a maintenance contract to ensure the continuous operation of the purchased application.

10.7.- Summary

- The three phases of the procurement process are need recognition, contract formalization, and contract administration.
- During the recognition of the need, the projects to be acquired are defined, and the specifications of what is sought to be acquired are prepared.
- Formalization of the contract is generally a very rigid process managed by areas specialized in negotiation or acquisitions.
- In formal organizations, such as public entities, where a rigorous set of laws governs procurement, more significant investments must be acquired via public bidding.
- During the execution of the contract, the project is developed.
- It is essential to formally evaluate the modifications to the project that may arise after signing the contract, as they may affect the cost or delivery time of the final project.
- The client is responsible for supervising that the product received meets the requested specifications and is complete with the manuals and training agreed upon in the contract.

10.8.- Review exercises

Questions

1. What are the three phases of the procurement process?
2. At what stage of the system lifecycle does need recognition occur?
3. Why is a specialized area needed in some organizations to formalize the contract?
4. What kind of follow-up should be given to the supplier during the execution of the contract?
5. What is change management, and why is it important?

Exercises

1. Find a technology contract on the Internet and identify the following:
   a. What is the object of the contract?
   b. Who are the parties?
   c. What are the clauses?
2. Look for the RFP of a public bidding process.
   a. What is being acquired?
   b. What are the events of the process and their dates?
   c. What are the requirements of the supplier?

Chapter 11

The Role of Technology Partners and Quality Certifications in the Operation

"Every individual necessarily labours to render the annual revenue of the society as great as he can. He generally, indeed, neither intends to promote the public interest, nor knows how much he is promoting it. ... he intends only his own gain, and he is in this, as in many other eases, led by an invisible hand to promote an end which was no part of his intention, nor is it always the worse for the society that it was no part of it. By pursuing his own interest, he frequently promotes that of the society more effectually than when he really intends to promote it."

Adam Smith, "The Wealth of Nations" 1776.

11.1.- Learning objectives

- Recognize the tools available from technology providers to support technology monitoring.
- Recognize the different roles that a technology partner can play in the definition, development, and operation of projects.
- Understanding the Value of Quality Certifications.
- Appreciate the value of treating colleagues with respect and honesty.

11.2.- The phases of the purchasing process

As discussed in previous chapters, purchasing a piece of hardware or software does not begin when a supplier is contacted or a request for proposal (RFP) is published. The process starts when the user, or IT, areas define the application required. Regardless of whether the solution is to build a new system, buy, or adapt a solution available in the market, the three phases of the procurement process are [Alanís, 2020]:

1. Recognition of the need
2. Formalization of the contract
3. Contract administration

Suppose a supplier learns about a project when an RFP is published (at the contract formalization stage). In that case, the tender specifications are likely for a different technology than their own or where they do not have a competitive advantage.

Technology providers need to seek to engage with their customers from the stage of recognition of the need to ensure that the solution the company plans to acquire fits the product the company is best prepared to supply. Additionally, this must be achieved without violating any laws, falling into conflicts of interest, or engaging in acts of corruption.

11.3.- Customer-supplier relationship in the pre-sales process

As discussed above, the purchasing process does not begin when a supplier is contacted or a request for proposal (RFP) is published. The process starts with the definition of the user's needs.

A supplier that learns of a project when an RFP is published (at the contract formalization stage) is probably too late to prepare a competitive bid. The requirements specifications could be for a technology from a different manufacturer, or it would not be easy to find a competitive advantage with the current specifications.

Technology providers must seek to engage with their customers from the stage of recognizing the need. This action will increase the chances that the solution the company plans to acquire fits the product the company is best prepared to supply. However, the customer-supplier relationship must not violate any law, create conflicts of interest, or involve acts of corruption.

In most cases, recognition of need begins with technology monitoring. In many companies, there is no specific area in charge of this function, or it belongs to a department usually short on resources and budget.

A win-win situation occurs when a company benefits from supplier visits and available documentation to support the technology monitoring efforts, while the supplier benefits by understanding the customer's needs early in the process. A provider may support the identification of opportunities with one or more of the following activities:

- Publication of information leaflets describing the technology
- Publication of case studies
- Organization of discussion groups
- Organization of conferences
- Visits to the technology areas of companies
- Relationship with user areas
- Publication of industry benchmarks
- Customer support in the preparation of bidding rules

Mini Case – We can buy any brand of equipment as long as it is the same as the model 6394 from this supplier.

Suppose a potential customer sends an RFP requesting pricing information for equipment of any brand. However, the description of the capabilities required copied the specifications of a competitor's computer. In that case, your competitor will likely have the advantage when it comes to offering products at better prices.

For example, an official RFP from a government office requested bids for computer equipment of any brand. The document specified that the equipment proposed had an Intel 6700 processor, four USB 3.0 ports, and a series of other specifications. The most interesting characteristic was that the equipment had to measure 50.8x30.5x5.08 centimeters and weigh exactly 2.7 kilograms.

If your company had worked with that potential customer before they released their RFP, the specifications might have been more general or the same as your product.

11.4.- Roles that technology partners can take

A technology service provider (whether hardware, software, applications, consulting, or solutions) can play different roles in its clients' IT projects. Sometimes the work can be in an advisory scheme for a fee; at other times, the work must be done without compensation, seeking either to strengthen a relationship of trust or a long-term benefit to sell a solution later.
The leading roles that a technology partner can occupy are:

- As an advisor
- As a technical supervisor of a project
- As a solution integrator
- As a developer or builder of a project or module

The detail of each role is described below.

As an advisor (paid or unpaid)

A company can become an advisor to an organization and provide recommendations, seek information, design solutions, or even train end users. The supplier can charge a fee (fixed price or on time and materials) or work at no cost to the client. The consulting company will not be able to get involved in the implementation of the projects it is advising or charge a "finder's fee" to the winning suppliers of said contracts. If the service is pro bono, the company can get involved in the implementation, competing with other providers in the procurement process. In that case, the consulting supplier would be expected to have an advantage because it knows the project better and would be better suited to the solutions it typically markets.

As a technical supervisor of a project (with payment)

A project's technical supervision involves supporting the organization in the recognition, formalization, and administration stages of a contract. In this role, the supplier company must represent the interests of the client organization. It would typically be a remunerated activity (either at a fixed price or on time and materials), and the technical supervisor would be prohibited from participating in the execution of the project to avoid a possible conflict of interest.

As a solution integrator (with payment)

The role of solution integrator is a well-defined function in information systems development practice. The complexity of the technologies and the variety of specialists required add to the relevance of the integrator's role. It is particularly relevant in organizations that need more specialized human resources with sufficient experience to guarantee the project's success. In some cases, the integrator subcontracts the services of the rest of the providers; in others, his function is to coordinate different companies.

The work of an integrator is remunerated, usually at a fixed price. The integrator assumes the risks of implementation problems and project malfunctions.

As a developer or builder of a project or module

Another well-recognized role in the industry is that of developer or builder of a project. This role is the same as solution integrator from the perspective charged for delivering a complete solution. Generally, company contracts are fixed-price contracts defined from the beginning of the project.

11.6.- International quality certifications and standards

Execution of IT plans is a significant issue for many organizations. Most ICT developments represent critical functions for the companies that hire them. However, developing these solutions is complex, costly, and highly dependent on the human factor.

A study of 8,000 software development projects in the U.S. found that 31% of them were canceled, 53% exceeded their costs by more than 180%, and only 9% of projects in large companies and 16% in small companies finished on time and on budget [Dominguez 2009].

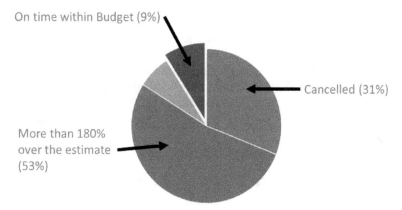

Figure 11.1 – Percentage of IT projects delivered on time and within budget [Dominguez, 2009]

Some studies show that following the proper steps can reduce development errors, ranging from 1.05 errors per thousand lines to 0.06 errors per thousand, and improve productivity that can reach up to 30% to 70%.

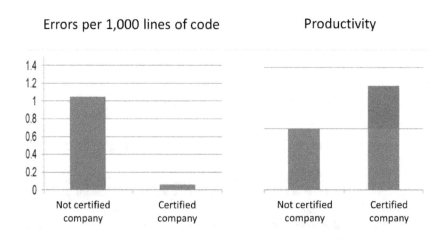

Errors per 1,000 lines of code   Productivity

Figure 11.2 – The value of certifications

A quality certificate is one in which a certification body declares the conformity of a product, service, or management system with a specific reference standard or process or a specialist's mastery over a particular technology.

Some of the benefits of having a quality certificate are:

- Possess a distinction of excellence from a recognized brand that customers seek.
- Differentiate yourself in a saturated market.
- Build credibility with your customers and suppliers.
- Execute your tasks with confidence and skill.
- Demonstrate your experience and expertise through a rigorous testing process.
- Possess a globally applicable accreditation that can lead to higher turnover rates.
- Demonstrate skills in leading, as well as executing, tasks and projects.

The results of applying the standards are so dramatic that, in some sectors, contracting companies look favorably on those suppliers that comply with these standards, going so far as to demand independent certification to ensure that the supplier meets specified quality standards (such as being CMM certified at a certain level or having a specific ISO certification).

Two critical challenges for Latin American IT companies that want to export their products or provide their services in local, U.S., or European markets are:

- to obtain the degree of quality required by these markets; and
- build credibility and trust from potential customers.

Table 11.1 – Different IT related certifications

MODEL	General use	SOURCE
COBIT	IT Objective control	ITGI (IT Governance Institute)
ITIM	IT investment management	GSA (General Services Administration)
Kano	Customer's needs and requirements	KANO
CMMI	Software development and integration	SEI (Software Engineering Institute)
Balanced Scorecard	Corporate measurements	Kaplan-Norton
e-Sourcing Capability Model	Sourcing	ITSQC (IT Services Qualification Center)
People - CMM (P-CMM)	Human resource management	SEI (Software Engineering Institute)
ISO 9001-2000	Quality management	ISO (International Standards Organization)
Six Sigma	Quality management and process improvement	Motorola
ISO / IEC 17799 & 27001	Security management	ISO (International Standards Organization)
ISO 20000 / BS 15000 / ITIL	IT infrastructure, service management, operations	ISO (International Standards Organization)
PMBOK / OPM3 / PMMM / PRINCE2	Project and program management	PMI (Project Management Institute)
OPBOX	Outsourcing	IAOP (International Association of Outsourcing)
Generic framework for IT management	IT Management	University of Amsterdam / Henderson & Venkatraman

General Model of Certifications:

A quality certification is one where a certificating body declares the conformity of a product, service, or management system with a specific reference standard or process or an individual's ability to exploit a particular technology.

There are two general groups of certifications:

- those that certify individuals and their skills and
- those that certify processes or organizations.

The basic process followed by individual certifications is the training of the individual and the accreditation of their knowledge through an examination or the documentation of individual capabilities.

In company certifications, the process generally includes the design of the procedures, their implementation, the inspection visits of an external certifying body, and the certification.

When it comes to certifying an individual's knowledge or skills, the steps are generally identifying the desired level of expertise, acquiring it (whether through courses, self-study, or professional experience), and validating that the knowledge is possessed at the expected level. The certification usually requires taking an exam, although there are cases where it is achieved by solving a practical problem or simply showing performance results on finished projects. The process varies depending on the type of technology and the needs of the certificating body.

Different institutions provide frameworks and even certifications in the different aspects of IT Corporate Governance. The following table adapted from Gad Selig's book "Implementing IT Governance" [Selig, 2008] shows different models, their applications, and the entity that issues them.

11.7.- The career of a technology specialist

During a specialist's professional development, they will likely change jobs, companies, and positions several times. It is common for a person to work for a technology services company as a supplier, serving customers in different areas. Then, through an agreement between their company and one of their customers, the specialists may be transferred to a production company and become a customer. Changes in the other direction also occur frequently.

From the supplier's point of view, it is essential to understand their customers' motivations and way of operating. Similarly, from the customer's point of view, knowing how their suppliers work can be an advantage when negotiating or looking for better solutions.

Finally, it is essential to treat colleagues respectfully and honestly, whether they are customers, suppliers, or competitors. That will make our discipline an area where it is a pleasure to work. Also, you never know if one day the positions could be reversed.

11.8.- Summary

- As discussed in previous chapters, the three phases of the procurement process are recognition of the need, formalization of the contract, and contract administration.
- Technology providers must seek to engage with their customers from the stage of recognizing the need, which begins with technology monitoring. Vendors can provide a series of activities for potential customers to aid in the identification of valuable technologies or opportunities for the organization.

- A provider may support identifying opportunities with activities such as organizing conferences or preparing case studies.
- During the lifecycle of a project, a technology supplier can play roles such as an advisor, a technical supervisor of a project, a solution integrator, or a developer or builder of a project or module.
- A quality certificate is one in which a certification body declares the conformity of a product, service, or management system with a specific reference standard or process or a specialist's mastery over a particular technology.
- Certifications can give a supplier recognition and a differentiating factor in competitive markets.

11.9.- Review exercises

Questions

1. What are the phases of the technology acquisition process?
2. At what stage of the technology acquisition process would it be in a vendor's best interest to engage with a potential customer?
3. What is an RFP?
4. What options are there, in addition to buying outright, to purchase technology from a supplier?
5. What roles can a technology partner play with a customer during the lifecycle of a project?

Exercises

1. Name five potential technology partners for a company.
2. Identify some possible presale activities (such as conferences, demonstrations, cases, etc.) from technology provider companies.
3. Research at least two certifications for companies in the area of technology development. Who grants them? What are they for? How are they obtained?
4. Search for an RFP from a technology client.
5. Identify an RFP that requires some quality certification from the vendor.
6. Locate at least two suppliers that have some quality certification.

Identify and describe at least two professional certifications that can be earned by a technology specialist and define the requirements for each.

Chapter 12

Emerging Technologies in Business Intelligence

"The very reason [the Greeks] got so far is that they knew how to pick up the spear and throw it onward from the point where others had left it. Their skill in the art of fruitful learning was admirable. We ought to be learning from our neighbors precisely as the Greeks learned from theirs, not for the sake of learned pedantry but rather using everything we learn as a foothold which will take us up as high, and higher, than our neighbor."

Friedrich Nietzsche, "Philosophy in the Tragic Age of the Greeks", 1873.

12.1.- Learning objectives

- Be able to interpret Gartner Hype Cycles.
- Identify business intelligence technologies in different stages of the Hype Cycle.
- Understand, in general terms, how Artificial Intelligence techniques work.
- Understand how Artificial Intelligence techniques can be used in industry applications.
- Understand how cryptocurrencies work.
- Know the advantages and disadvantages of using cryptocurrencies to exchange value.
- Analyze different applications of blockchain in the industry.

12.2 – Gartner Hype Cycles

Gartner Inc. It is a company founded in 1979 that provides research results and unbiased, vendor-agnostic guidance about technology to specialists in IT and other areas in organizations [Gartner, 2024]. Two of the company's most consulted products include magic quadrants and hype cycles.

Magic quadrants analyze different companies and products based on their Completeness of vision and ability to execute, concentrating on specific technologies. A magic quadrant categorizes participants as leaders, challengers, visionaries, or niche players.

Hype cycles map the cycle of maturity, adoption, and social application of different technologies on a graph. The graphs categorize the products into five groups:

"Technology trigger" – Where the presentation of the product generates interest.

"Peak of inflated expectations" - The impact on the media usually generates enthusiasm and unrealistic expectations. Some success stories and many failures can be seen.

"Trough of disillusionment" - Not all expectations are met, and some technologies are discarded. Investment continues only when the product is improved to meet early adopters' expectations.

"Slope of enlightenment" – Some benefits have started to materialize, and more companies are supporting prototypes to understand the benefits that the practical application of technology can provide.

"Plateau of productivity" – The benefits of technology are widely demonstrated and accepted. Technology is becoming more and more stable and evolving in second and third generations. Mainstream adoption starts.

The cycle also marks whether a technology is expected to be developed in the next 2, 5, 10, or more years.

The "Hype Cycle for Analytics and Business Intelligence, 2023" is the Gartner report number G00792723, published in July 2023 [Macari and Krensky, 2023].

12.3.- Business intelligence technologies at different stages of the hype cycle

Technology on the Plateau of Productivity
There is only one technology on the plateau of productivity. It is expected to have a maturation horizon of less than two years: *Predictive Analytics*, which uses statistical techniques to answer questions about what is likely to happen. According to Gartner, many companies have initiatives in this area, and there is a growing interest in the subject.

Technologies on the Slope of Enlightenment
There are four technologies at this stage. Two of them have a maturity horizon of two years: Event Stream Processing (computing performed on streaming data to attain situation awareness) and Cloud Analytica (tools to deliver analytical capabilities as a service).

Two technologies at this stage have a horizon of two to five years: *Self-Service Analytics* (technology that allows end users to process data) and *Embedded Analytics* (analytics delivered to a user without needing to change applications).

Technologies in earlier stages
One technology in this group has a maturation horizon of less than two years (*Natural Language Query*). All others are expected to mature between 2 and 5 years or 5 to 10 years. These include Prescriptive Analytics, Data and Analytics Governance, and Natural Language Generation.

12.4.- What is artificial intelligence?

When people think of artificial intelligence (AI), the first thing that comes to mind is some science fiction movies where machines take control of the planet and destroy humanity. The name is misleading. Artificial intelligence does not refer to creating thinking entities but to using programming techniques that copy human reasoning processes to maximize the chances of reaching their goal [Simon, 1981].

Among the techniques used in artificial intelligence systems are rule processing, computational learning, genetic algorithms, natural language recognition, and computer vision.

For example, a simple game is the game of tic-tac-toe (three in a row, noughts and crosses, Xs and Os, or gato as it is known in different countries), a game on a board of 3 x 3 spaces where opponents take turns marking a box and whoever gets three matching symbols on the same line wins (either vertical, horizontal, or diagonal). If we wanted to program a computer to play the game, there are several alternatives:

Algorithms

The first option would be to register all possible games in sequence. If the sequence is small, all possible answers can be calculated. An algorithm is a finite, well-defined sequence of instructions. If the number of moves is finite, this solution would work well. However, a game with one or two more lines on the board would make the number of alternatives enormous, making this method impossible to follow. To solve these problems, you are looking for a good enough solution, although there might be better options.

Rules

When you can't define all the steps to follow in advance, one way to attack the problem is to create general rules and check them to determine if a condition is met. In tic-tac-toe, for example, you can define specific general rules and ask the computer to review those rules on each move:

1. If the opponent has three marks in a line finish (lose)
2. If I have two tiles on a line and there is a free space on that line, occupy the space and finish (win)
3. If there are no free spaces on the board, finish (tie)
4. If the opponent has two marks on a line that has a space, occupy the space
5. If occupying a space creates two rows with two of my tiles and a space in each, take that space.
6. ... (here are several more rules)
7. If no rule applies, place the mark in any available space.

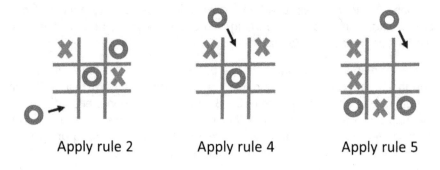

Apply rule 2   Apply rule 4   Apply rule 5

Figure 12.1 – Example of applying rules in a tic-tac-toe game.

An expert system playing a board game could apply a series of rules according to the board's conditions. These programs are called expert systems because an expert would know and apply those rules. However, today, we understand that an expert, besides the known rules, uses intuition and experience when deciding his courses of action. Therefore, an expert system is generally only as good as a novice (with all the theory but little experience).

Computer or machine learning

Another technique to solve the board game problem would be to list the conditions that define a winning game, a draw, and a losing game and then prepare a program that plays any available move during its turn but stores the choices made. If a move used before leads to a loss more times than a win, then it should be avoided. If a move has led to victory more times, it can be repeated.

With enough games played, there would be information as to which move has the best chance of leading to a win, given the current conditions of the board. It could be said that a program "learned" which plays works best [Bishop, 2006].

Genetic algorithms

In nature, a being has a specific genetic code that gives it the characteristics necessary to survive. During reproduction, a new genetic code is generated in a new being through the combination of genes and some random variations that may occur. If this new combination and variations make the new individual more likely to survive, that code will reproduce more and be more prevalent; those genetic modifications that do not help survival will tend to be eliminated by nature.

A genetic algorithm [Mitchel, 1996] works in much the same way. A route to fix a problem is generated. An element in that path can then be randomly modified. If the modification achieves a better solution, that new route is established as the basis, and the evolutionary process continues. If the change doesn't help, it's scrapped and reverted to the old code. Again, a reasonably adequate solution to a complex problem can be found after enough attempts.

Natural Language Processing

Another sub-area of artificial intelligence is the processing and understanding of natural language to carry out translations, answer questions, gather news, or interpret correspondence. The process consists of dividing sentences into their components (subject-verb-complement) and categorizing each section. Natural language processing has been studied since the early days of commercial computers [Borbow, 1964; Schank, 1972]. However, the complexity of the problem required high volumes of processing and storage that were only available recently. Today, it is expected to talk to systems that recognize natural language and interpret instructions, such as Siri (from Apple) or Alexa (from Amazon).

12.5.- The use of artificial intelligence techniques in other disciplines

Artificial Intelligence in Medical Diagnostics

Building an expert system to play tic-tac-toe may sound trivial, but it is possible to find the rules for a medical diagnosis, for example, and program them into an expert system. The system would not give a precise diagnosis. Still, based on known rules, it can list some diseases and the probability according to the picture the patient presents regarding symptoms, personal data, and history.

For example, a rule group might start like this:
1. If a patient has a fever, they may have influenza.
2. But if you also have a wound, then it's more likely that the fever is caused by an infection caused by a reaction to the wound.
3. ... (many more rules would go here)

The system would review the rules and could indicate the likelihood of different diseases. With enough rules, you can create an expert system for medical diagnosis, which is a system that emulates the steps a medic follows when diagnosing a patient. An expert system can diagnose as well as a beginner (as mentioned above) because it follows the basic rules. Still, it brings the expert closer to the data and allows them to decide what other information to review to complete a final diagnosis.

Artificial Intelligence in Accounting

In the same way that expert systems can be programmed to play tic-tac-toe or chess or to make medical diagnoses, they can also process rules to detect unusual transactions on a credit card. The system could analyze thousands of transactions, and those that deviate from a client's "normal" pattern can be flagged for processing by a human to detect possible fraud.

Auditing is another possible use of expert systems. With the proper rules, a system can flag inconsistent or incomplete documents. Moreover, an automated system can review 100% of a company's documents instead of a smaller percentage (which is the standard procedure when conducting an audit).

Natural language processing systems can be used to process customer emails and define whether the message needs to be attended to by a human urgently or waiting for their turn. These systems can even generate a statistic of the topics covered in the emails received and identify how happy or angry the customers who wrote are (in a process called sentiment analysis). They can also analyze contracts, identify keywords, find inconsistencies, or make recommendations.

Although the idea of using technology to support accounting and auditing is not new [Keenoy, 1958], recent advances and the availability of technology have allowed accounting firms to make significant developments and suggest that their impact will be greater in the future. Some systems currently in use include a partnership between KPMG and IBM's Watson AI platform to develop AI-powered auditing tools; PricewaterhouseCoopers' (PwC) Halo, a platform for AI products; and Deloitte's Argus for AI, and Optix for data analytics. [Kokina & Davenport, 2017].

In the future, Artificial Intelligence (AI) "will help accountants find correlations and patterns in their data that legacy solutions could not have previously identified. Hopefully, new insights into your data will lead to a better trading strategy. AI is already transforming the profession; I would even say reinventing it, with advancements such as RPA [Robotics Process Automation] and the automation of lower-level decision-making, transaction processing, fraud detection, and much more" [English, 2019].

Minicase – Discovering fraud by finding an unusual number in the movie "The Accountant."

In the 2016 film "The Accountant," starring Ben Affleck and Anna Kendrick, the accountant discovers fraud by reviewing the company's books for the last 15 years and noticing that certain transactions all have the number 3 as the second digit. In that scene, the accountant discovers everything with his superior mental abilities, but could an expert system have helped detect these kinds of suspicious movements in real life? Could a computer review hundreds of moves and show which ones require a (human) specialist to perform a detailed review?

12.6.- Cryptocurrencies

An additional emerging technology that has raised interest for its great potential to change the way markets work and even the way we live is cryptocurrencies (or electronic money).

Let's assume that Alice wants to send Bob money for a bicycle she bought from him. Alice can take money to him personally, deposit money into Bob's bank account, send him a money order, or mail a check.

However, if they live in different cities, and there is no bank with branches in both places, or there is no time to wait for a letter, the alternatives become complicated. One option would be to pay Bob electronically using the Internet.

The problem is that the Internet is a public network, which means that if Alice sends a message to Bob, this message will travel through many computers until it reaches its destination. Anyone with the right technology can read the message or even change it. Sending a message over the Internet is like sending it on the radio; we hope it reaches its destination, but nothing stops someone else from seeing it.

Sending money securely online can be tricky. I can't send cash; it doesn't travel electronically. Two possible solutions are using a trusted intermediary (a bank) or directly sending electronic money.

Sending money using a bank as a trusted intermediary

The first alternative to pay Bob is to use an intermediary that both parties trust (a bank) to keep the accounts and know how much Alice has. Alice sends her credit card number to Bob, who requests authorization from the bank to charge; if the bank approves it, Bob trusts that the bank will pay him, while the bank trusts that it can charge Alice. Of course, the card number can't travel directly over the Internet. Anyone with some practice can intercept and read a message on the network. That's why it is necessary to encrypt (encrypt or scramble) the credit card number. That is, modifying the number using a key (for example, Alice can add 3 to each card digit and then send Bob the resulting number). Bob can decrypt (decrypt or decode) the number and proceed with the charge (in this example, Bob would have to subtract three from each digit he receives to have the correct credit card number). Anyone who sees the card number sent during the transmission would see an incorrect number. In this case, both participants use a single key, a shared key.

The problem is that the bank takes a fee (which it charges Bob), and the transaction takes some time. Additionally, the transaction can be canceled after Bob has delivered the bicycle if Alice tells the bank that the transaction is fake and that she never made any transaction with Bob. In that case, Bob could be left without a bicycle and money.

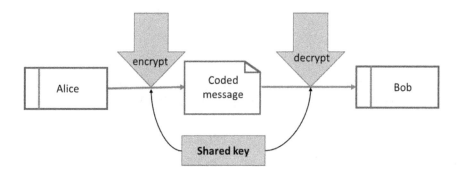

Figure 12.2 - Encryption with a shared key.

Sending e-money over the Internet

The other option is for Alice to send Bob electronic money via e-mail. Electronic money (or cryptocurrencies) is a sequence of numbers people assign value to. To buy a cryptocurrency, a person can pay real money (Fiat money like Dollars, Euros, or Pesos) and receive a sequence of numbers. Similarly, a person can sell their cryptocurrency (or part of it) and receive cash, products, or services in exchange for it.

The advantage of this alternative is that you don't have to use an intermediary that charges a high commission. If done correctly, the money is sent immediately (there is no waiting time), and the transaction is irreversible (once Alice sends the money, there is no backing up). Once Bob receives the money, he knows that the money is already his.

Another advantage of electronic currency is that it can be handled anonymously, the same as cash, without the recipient having to know the name, card number, and credit history of the issuer.

Electronic money is a sequence of numbers that can travel over the Internet. There are two problems to solve with electronic money: how to make sure that no one else can spend it (someone who can intercept the message) and how to assure the recipient that I can't use the same money twice (if Alice sends the code to Bob, what stops Alice from sending the same code to someone else).

How does the owner of the electronic money ensure that no one else can spend that same currency?

The first part is solved by encrypting the electronic money so that no one knows the correct sequence of numbers. Encryption is achieved with a double set of keys. When Alice bought her cryptocurrency, she had two encryption keys: one that everyone can see (public key) and one that only she knows (private key).

The public and private keys package is generated with a mathematical formula such that:

- It is not possible to guess one key by having the other, and,
- What is encrypted with one of these keys can only be decrypted with the other.
- So, if something is encrypted with Alice's public key, only her private key can decrypt it.

When Alice buys a coin, the coin is encrypted using Alice's public key. Since she is the only one who knows her private key, there is a certainty that only she can spend that electronic money since only she can decipher it to use it. No matter how many people see the encrypted money, they can't use it.

For Alice to pay Bob, she has to decrypt her currency using her private key, encrypt the currency using Bob's public key, and send the resulting code to Bob over the Internet. Now, the coin belongs to Bob, and only he can spend it. If someone else sees that message with the coin, they won't be able to use it because only Bob knows his private key, which is the only key that can open that coin. Additionally, upon receiving it, Bob knows it is his currency and no one else's since it is encrypted with his public key.

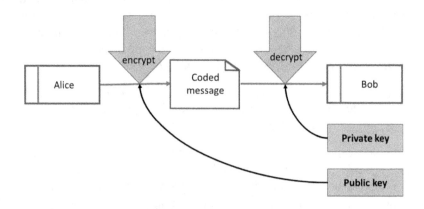

Figure 12.3 - Private and public key encryption.

Sometimes, the transaction amount may be different from one entire electronic coin. Alice can divide the coin into fractions and pay a portion of a coin (e.g., a quarter of her cryptocurrency). She has to decrypt her cryptocurrency, divide the resulting code into parts, assign certain parts to the coin she will send to Bob (encrypting that part with Bob's public key), and encrypt the remaining part of the coin with Alice's public key. That way, part of the coin now belongs to Bob and the other part to Alice.

How do we assure the recipient of electronic currency that the money sent to them will not be mailed to someone else as well?

Sending the same money to two recipients is known as double-spending. And it could be done if Alice were a little dishonest because she can decipher her currency, make a copy of it (after all, it's just a sequence of numbers), and encrypt a copy with Bob's public key and another copy with Charles' public key.

A solution to avoid double spending is to encode every transaction made with a particular coin into a ledger book. This book includes the history of all the transactions made to that coin, from the moment it was created (minted) to the present. If you go through the list of transactions from the beginning, you can know who owns what percentage of the coin now. (What is known is which key controls the currency, though not necessarily who owns the key.) If someone wants to use a key to open the coin, by going through the list of transactions, you can find out if that key has a balance, that is, if that expense can be made or not.

Keeping track of who owns which coin requires keeping a ledger (a book) with each transaction made on each coin, a book that says how much money each person has in their accounts. The question is, who can be trusted to keep that ledger? Instead of one bank maintaining the accounts, many copies of the ledger are created, and everyone (or many) can keep everyone's accounts simultaneously (known as a distributed ledger). If someone spends something, that is updated in all books. So, if Alice spends her money, everyone knows that coin (or portion of a coin) no longer exists; now, there's a new coin with Bob's key. And if Alice tries to send a copy of the money to Carlos, that copy would be rejected because, in the account books (which everyone has), they already know that that key no longer has a balance, preventing it from being used twice. This strategy depends on having a distributed ledger (with copies in the hands of many participants).

How are distributed ledgers kept up to date?

A cryptocurrency's ledger of accounts is kept in a structure known as a blockchain. A block is a group of transactions placed in a package, and the packages are placed in sequences or chains. Each package includes a hash number (verification code). When the hash number and the numbers of all the elements in the package are applied to a formula, the resulting number is a recognizable value (like 000). It is easy to verify if a hash number is correct; if anything on the package changes, the numbers and the key will not add to the expected result. Hash numbers are easy to verify but laborious to calculate.

Each package includes a link to the preceding package (and that package's verification code), the transactions to be added to the chain, and a verification key. Suppose someone changes anything in the previous package or any of the earlier packages. In that case, the link of the last package or the verification key will not match its expected value, and the string will be rejected. This type of structure allows information to be added to a string without being able to modify any of the previous data.

When Alice sends a cryptocurrency to Bob, this transaction is added to a list of transactions to be confirmed. Once every ten minutes (the time varies depending on the currency we are using), a group of companies compete to take the pending transactions and add a new block that is added to the chain. Adding new blocks to the chain is complicated because it requires a lot of computing power to calculate the verification keys and form the latest package. The company that can do those calculations first publishes the new block to be added to the list and transmits it to all stakeholders (updating the ledger), passed between the nodes. If someone else tries to publish a new version of that block, it would be rejected by the nodes that have the ledger because they already have that node in their lists. Companies dedicated to creating new nodes are called miners because every time they generate a new node, they also produce a new coin (or part of a coin) that they receive as payment for their services.

Miners need powerful equipment to perform mathematical operations faster than their competitors. A miner receives income by creating new coins in each block built (but that amount will eventually be reduced so that in a few years, no more coins can be made). A miner also receives income as a fee that Alice can add to her transaction (such as a tip to the miner) for including her transaction in the block. If there are too many pending transactions, a miner will take the ones offering the most commission and process them in the current block; the others will have to wait for another cycle.

Transactions typically take up to six cycles to be written to all distributed ledgers. In the case of a significant transaction, it may be convenient to wait a reasonable time (6 to 20 cycles) to be 100% sure that the transaction was firm and irrevocably recorded in all books. In contrast, small transactions can be trusted that, with one or two cycles, are safe if the transaction has already been recorded; there is little chance that someone will attack the network to kill a small transaction, so it can be considered safe.

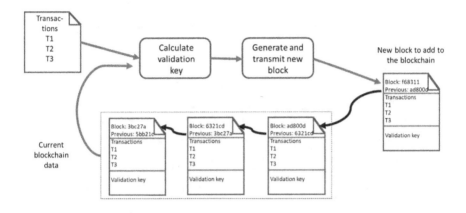

Figure 12.4 - Creating a new block in a blockchain.

12.7.- Types of cryptocurrencies

The first functional cryptocurrency is Bitcoin, which was created by a person (or group of people) known as Satoshi Nakamoto and published in a white paper [Nakamoto 2008].

A Bitcoin is a cryptocurrency based on transactions between individuals (it does not require a central bank) and stored on a blockchain, creating a distributed ledger. A community of miners competes (through a process known as proof-of-work) to add new transactions to the chain and, at the same time, create new bitcoins.

The number of bitcoins created by each new node (and paid to miners) decreases over time; when 21 million bitcoins have been minted (around the year 2140), new coins will no longer be produced, and miners will have to live only on the transaction fees offered by the market.

Each bitcoin can be divided into small parts called Satoshis, after the currency's creator. One bitcoin is divided into 100 million Satoshis.

The value of cryptocurrencies fluctuates in the market. By multiplying the available coins by market price, you can identify the cryptocurrencies with the highest capitalization. Since the cost of cryptocurrencies is constantly changing, you can check the latest value and capitalization of each coin at the following link: https://finance.yahoo.com/crypto/

Table 12.1 – Cryptocurrencies with highest market cap (February 2024)
[Yahoo, 2024]

Name	Market Cap
Bitcoin	843,890 Billions USD
Ethereum	276,674 Billions USD
Tether	96,195 Billions USD
BNB USD	44,961 Billions USD
Solana	43,406 Billions USD
XRP USD	27,735 Billions USD

Minicase - Who is Satoshi Nakamoto?

The first functional cryptocurrency is Bitcoin, which was created by Satoshi Nakamoto and published in a white paper [Nakamoto 2008]. The funny thing is that Satoshi Nakamoto is a pseudonym, and no one knows if it is one person or several, nor is his identity known. That person published the article explaining how Bitcoin works and participated in technical discussions, collaborating with platform developers until 2010. It transferred control of the domains and codes to community members on that date and disappeared. No one knows Satoshi Nakamoto's whereabouts.

12.8.- Other Blockchain Applications

Cryptocurrencies are just one of the possible uses of blockchains. Having an instrument to which information can be added, identifying who added it, and not allowing any of the above data to be modified can be helpful in many disciplines. Some possible applications are:

Updating and transmitting medical records: Different doctors can update a patient's record; the chain keeps track of who and how the record has been revised, and all interested parties can see the patient's current status.

Shared ownership: A valuable painting can have multiple owners. Ownership can be defined as a chain, and owners can pass on their shares in whole or in part to other owners. Who owns the artwork is determined by the current state of the chain.

Ownership of a company: In the same way a painting can have several owners, a company can distribute its shares as a cryptocurrency. The initial offering is an ICO (Initial Coin Offering), and buyers can then negotiate the sale of their percentages by transferring all or part of their coins (as is done with shares in the physical world). Dividends and voting rights can be distributed according to the percentage of ownership defined on the chain at the time of the decision.

Keeping a product's distribution chain safe: Food can be tracked from when it is produced until it reaches the consumer. Suppose any segment of the supply chain has a health issue. In that case, it is possible to immediately identify all the food that passes through that station and stop it before it reaches the final consumer.

Electronic voting: With blockchain, you can ensure that people vote only once and that all votes are counted.

There are countless possible applications, and the list is constantly updated; some articles about blockchain applications can be found on the sites of accounting firms and technology developers. Table 12.2 shows some examples.

Table 12.2 – Web pages with information about blockchain applications

Company	Internet address
PWC	https://www.pwc.com/gx/en/industries/assets/blockchain-technology-in-energy.pdf
Deloitte	https://www2.deloitte.com/content/dam/Deloitte/in/Documents/strategy/in-strategy-innovation-blockchain-revolutionary-change-noexp.pdf
KPMG	https://home.kpmg/xx/en/home/insights/2017/02/digital-ledger-services-at-kpmg-fs.html
EY	https://www.ey.com/en_gl/blockchain
IBM	https://www.ibm.com/blockchain/use-cases/
Microsoft	https://azure.microsoft.com/en-us/solutions/blockchain/
Hewlett Packard	https://www.hpe.com/us/en/solutions/blockchain.html

The effective use of blockchain can offer several benefits, including non-repudiation of transaction data, cost savings through disintermediation, and a verifiable chain of custody. However, other concerns, such as end-user security, the ability to recover lost keys, and the inability to correct or undo a transaction, make it difficult to commercialize this technology fully." [Cieslak, Mason & Vetter, 2019].

12.9.- Summary

- Gartner Inc. It is a company founded in 1979 dedicated to providing research results information to specialists in technology and other areas in organizations [Gartner, 2021].
- The company's products include magic quadrants and hype cycles.
- Different business intelligence technologies can be identified at various stages of the hype cycle.
- Artificial intelligence (AI) refers to programming techniques that copy a human's steps to maximize the chances of reaching their goal.
- Some AI techniques are expert systems, computer learning, genetic algorithms, and natural language processing.
- Electronic Money (or cryptocurrencies) is a sequence of numbers people assign value to.
- In the world of cryptocurrencies, a miner is a company that validates transactions made with cryptocurrencies, creates new coins, and

adds a node with the transactions to the blockchain that forms the distributed ledger.

- Other blockchain applications can be found in finance, medical records, supply chains, and e-voting.

12.10.- Review exercises

Questions

1. Mention some Artificial Intelligence techniques.
2. What does an expert system do?
3. How can an expert system be helpful in the audit process?
4. What use can a natural language recognition system have in accounting practice?
5. What is a cryptocurrency?
6. What is a blockchain?
7. He mentions some advantages and disadvantages of using cryptocurrencies to exchange value
8. What is shared key encryption?
9. How does public-key and private-key encryption work?
10. How do I make sure no one can spend one of my crypto?
11. How do you guarantee the receiver of a cryptocurrency that the sender can't double-spend?
12. What is the role of a miner in the cryptocurrency environment?
13. Who is Satoshi Nakamoto?

Exercises

1. Fin Find an example of an expert system used in accounting.
2. Among the list of rules that appear in the chapter for playing tic-tac-toe, point number 6 indicates that some rules need to be added. Complete the rules that would go at that point to ensure the best performance in the game by reviewing those rules from top to bottom on each play.
3. Research some blockchain applications in the industry that have yet to be mentioned in this book.
4. Research what it takes to buy a Bitcoin (or some Satoshis) and how much it costs.

Module V

Next Steps for Business Intelligence

Chapter 13

Managing the Introduction of Technological Innovations in Organizations

"Here, we have to bear in mind that nothing is harder to organize, more likely to fail, or more dangerous to see through than the introduction of a new system of government. The person bringing in the changes will make enemies of everyone who was doing well under the old system, while the people who stand to gain from the new arrangements will not offer wholehearted support, ... people are naturally skeptical: no one really believes in change until they've had the solid experience of it."

Niccolò Machiavelli, "The Prince" (Chapter VI), 1532.

13.1.- Learning objectives

- Identify the characteristics of an innovation.
- Defining Business Intelligence as an Innovation.
- Identify the phases and steps in adopting innovations by individuals and organizations.
- Describe the process of adopting an innovation.
- Identify the type of support required by users and departments during the different stages of the innovation adoption process.
- Know the activities that can accelerate or stop the adoption of innovations.

13.2.- Business intelligence as innovation

Innovation is an idea, practice, or object perceived as new to an individual or an organization [Rogers, 2003]. The solution may have been around for some time; Other groups may even use it. However, for that individual, an innovation is something they face for the first time, or that wasn't considered practical or convenient given the conditions they faced when the opportunity last appeared.

Using Rogers' definition, almost any business intelligence system is an innovation. An activity may have existed in one form or another in the company but not at the level and speed it shows now.

For a specialist who wants to try new techniques or a manager who wants to help their employees do their best, it's a good idea to study how innovations behave in organizations. It's valuable to understand the kind of help pioneers need and to know what to expect when people are asked to try something new.

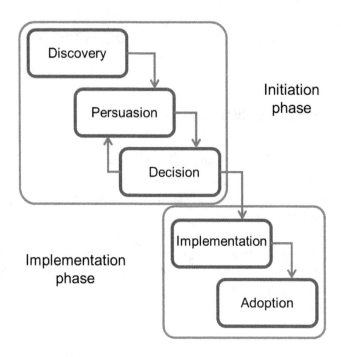

Figure 13.1 - Stages of the innovation adoption process (Adapted from [Alanis 1991; Rogers 2003])

13.3.- The evolution of the process of adopting innovations

Innovations do not appear or are adopted simultaneously by all members of an organization. There are always groups that accept them first, and some laggards still would never use the new solutions.

The graph of the number of people who gradually take up an innovation usually forms a bell-shaped curve or, in statistical terms, a standard distribution curve [Brancheau 1987]. The chart allows people to identify five groups of users, depending on how quickly they decide to adopt the innovation. Figure 13.2 shows this distribution.

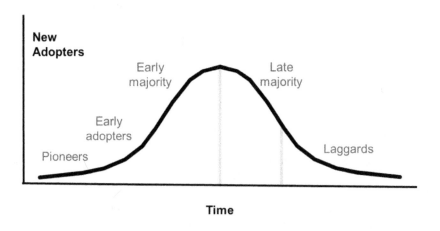

Figura 13.2 – Distribution of innovators

With any innovation, you can always find people who use and adopt it before anyone else. They are the pioneers. A pioneer likes to try new devices and ideas, even if they don't generate any additional value. This group requires little support. They usually move toward innovations on their own. Sometimes, even too fast. In the old adventure movies, the pioneers were the ones who came back from the desert with arrows on their backs. But their job was to blaze trails and find opportunities.

The most important group is the early adopters. They look at the pioneers, and if they find essential value in an innovation, they embrace it. The group is vital because once the early adopters have chosen something, it's only a matter of time before the rest of the group accepts it. Early adopters require access to pioneers and direct support to simplify their decision to embrace innovation.

The group that follows early adopters has two subgroups: early majority and late majority, depending on whether they adopt innovation before or after the 50% mark. In this group, growth is rapid. Users in this group do not need special incentives to embrace new technologies. Still, the company needs to expand its facilities and capabilities to accommodate the demand for resources that this growing number of users needs.

The last group is the laggards. They only adopt an innovation once it is thoroughly tested or forced to do so. As with any change, there's always someone who will never adopt it, and it's normal not to worry too much about that group.

Minicase - Not all innovations are successful, even if they come from the same company.

In November 2017, when Apple was about to launch the iPhone X, customers who wanted to buy the phone formed long lines outside stores even a day before its launch [Wuerthele, 2017]. A year later, in September 2018, armies of Apple fans formed long lines to be the first to buy the iPhone XS and iPhone XS Max [Hein, 2018]. However, not all of Apple's products have been successful. In August 1993, Apple released the Newton, a handheld computer that would be the forerunner of PDAs, tablets and smartphones. However, the device was costly, heavy, and flawed. By February 1998, the Newton had been discontinued [Gilbert & Varanasi, 2023; Gallagher, 2023]

13.4.- The support required by a technological innovation over time

While Figure 13.2 shows the number of new people adopting a technology, Figure 13.3 shows the total number of people who have already adopted it at any given time. This chart is essential because it shows the number of users taking advantage of the technology by a specific date and can be used to estimate the type of effort needed to support those groups.

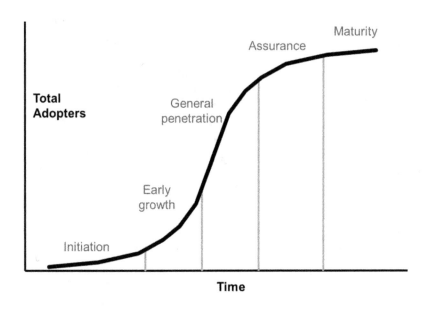

Figure 13.3 - Innovation maturity model

In the curve in Figure 13.3, five stages in the adoption process can be identified. During the startup stage, there are few users, but they require support on an individual basis. Sometimes, they need some help convincing themselves of the value of the new product. For innovation to be adopted, it is necessary at this stage to absorb the risks of acquiring technology by providing users with subsidies and direct support to facilitate their decision to adopt new solutions.

As some users see the value of technology, more and more users are adopting it. In the initial growth phase, subsidies are less significant, as innovation has already proven its value, but it becomes increasingly more challenging to support all users personally. At this stage, it's essential to convey the responsibility and risk of adoption to users and pave the way for rapid growth during the overall penetration phase. The danger at this stage is that there needs to be more resources to provide direct personal support to all new users. Many users would want to innovate and need help to be supported. This situation causes tension and puts the project's future at risk, as many users might give up on adopting the innovation simply because the waiting list is too long. Figure 13.4 illustrates this phenomenon.

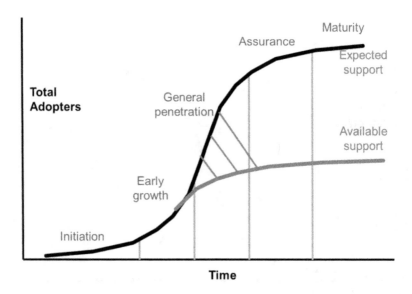

Figure 13.4 - Lack of growth due to over-control of innovation in the early growth stage

The organization should prepare to support many users quickly after the early growth phase. Users can accept some adoption risks, but they will need support for the features of this new technology. Services such as training, helpdesk, and technical support must work efficiently if most users are to embrace innovation.

Another point of risk occurs in the shift to the maturity phase.

The number of new users stopped growing (as almost everyone has embraced the innovation), and although technical support must continue, it must no longer grow, as demand is now stable. The danger at this stage is not seeing this stop in demand and continuing to expand the services available, spending more than necessary on support.

It is essential that support services mature and stabilize upon reaching maturity to ensure continued support for the technology without incurring unnecessary costs. Figure 13.5 illustrates uncontrolled growth and shows the distance between the required support level and the level offered, which would indicate overspending.

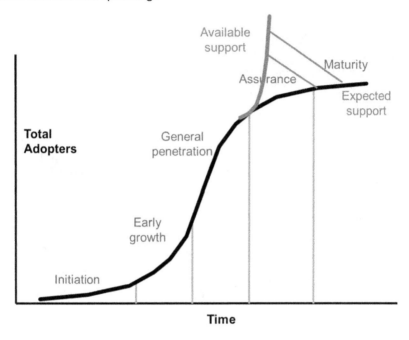

Figure 13.5 - Overspending by not stopping accelerated growth in innovation support in time

13.5.- Controlling the speed of adoption of technological innovations

The healthy growth of technological innovation in an organization requires different types of support at its various stages of maturation. As shown in Figure 13.6, the technology adoption process has three very distinct phases, each requiring a different type of support. An organization may decide to increase the support needed to speed up the adoption process or (if it doesn't have a budget or doesn't match its strategy) stop the required support, slowing down the speed with which an innovation is received.

During the early stages, the innovation is being analyzed by a small group of pioneers. They usually only require a little technical support. They almost always get their information from sources outside the organization, and their knowledge is greater than that of specialists in the areas of support that the company may have. A group of pioneers with independent budgets to research new technologies and a reward system for finding meaningful technologies can speed up discovering innovations applicable to the organization. Some organizations have even gone so far as to create areas responsible for monitoring technologies to support this process. On the other hand, limiting the budget and even punishing failed attempts to acquire useful technology can block or completely stop the introduction of innovations in an organization.

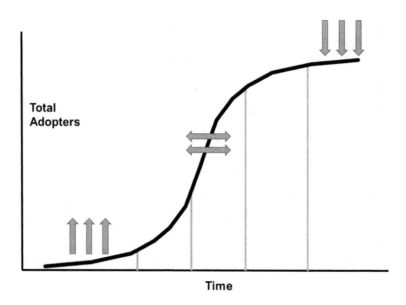

Figure 13.6 - Type of support needed at the different stages of maturation of an innovation.

Once the pioneers have discovered an exciting innovation, the group of early innovators becomes the focus of attention.

This group requires a more evident justification for accepting innovation. Introducing strategies to reduce innovation's direct and indirect costs can tilt the cost/benefit balance in favor of adoption for this group. One way to reduce costs is by purchasing the necessary equipment with a central rather than departmental budget, establishing a technical support area, and looking for ways to reward the additional efforts needed to test the technology.

When most people have decided to adopt the technology, direct financial support is no longer a priority because, at this stage, innovation has already proven its value. The budget should now be geared towards providing better support structures and simplifying the process for acquiring the innovation so that innovation moves through this phase as soon as possible.

As the company reaches the maturity stage, growing support services is no longer necessary as the demand for innovation slows down. Most people have already embraced innovation. The important thing at this stage is to standardize and apply rules to make the process of using innovation more economical.

13.6.- Management of multiple innovations

Every innovation has its S-shaped curve. Some technological solutions have taken faster paths than others, and this depends on many factors.

Managing multiple innovations in a company requires various curves, different support needs, and different levels of penetration in the organization. A good manager must distinguish the support required at each stage for each innovation and act according to the specific needs and objectives that the organization wishes to achieve. Figure 13.7 illustrates the management of different technologies at any given time within an organization [Alanis, 2010].

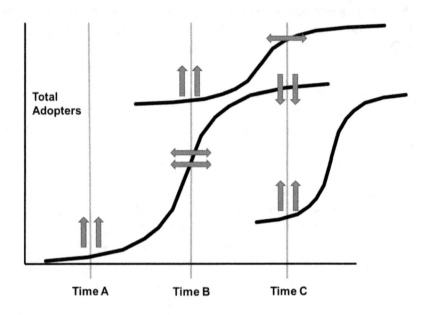

Figure 13.7 - Support required by different innovations at different points.

13.7.- Summary

- An innovation is an idea, practice, or object perceived as new to an individual or an organization.
- Almost any business intelligence system is an innovation.
- The innovation adoption process has two phases: initiation and implementation.
- During the initiation phase, the user identifies and studies the innovation. The user forms a favorable or unfavorable attitude towards the product and decides to adopt or reject it. The steps are discovery, persuasion, and adoption.
- The implementation phase begins when the user buys or starts using the proposed product and concludes when the innovation becomes routine. The steps are implementation and adoption.
- Innovations do not appear or are adopted simultaneously by all members of an organization. There are always groups that accept them first, and some laggards still would never use the new solutions. The groups can be categorized as pioneers, early innovators, early majority, late majority, and laggards.

- The number of users who have adopted an innovation determines the type and amount of support needed. The maturation process of an innovation follows five stages: initiation, early growth, overall penetration, assurance, and maturity.

13.8.- Review exercises

Questions

1. What is an innovation?
2. Why can it be argued that information technologies are innovations?
3. What are the phases of the individual process of adopting an innovation?
4. What behavior identifies pioneers in an innovation?
5. What behavior characterizes the early majority in an innovation?
6. Why are early adopters essential for innovation?
7. Why are different types of support required depending on what stage of maturity an innovation is at within the company?
8. At what stage of the innovation curve would you place smartphone use in a company?

Exercises

1. Identify a business intelligence system and explain why it can be considered an innovation.
2. Identify a recent technological innovation that has not reached the stage of general penetration.
3. Identify a product that is in the startup stage.
4. Identify a technology that is in the early growth stage.
5. Identify a Mature Technology.

Chapter 14

The Future of Information Technology and its Impact on Business

"Before I draw nearer to that stone to which you point," said Scrooge, "answer me one question. Are these the shadows of the things that Will be, or are they shadows of things that May be, only?"

Charles Dickens, "A Christmas Carol," 1843

14.1.- Learning objectives

- Appreciate the speed at which technology changes.
- Understand that a vision of the future is forged by understanding how we got to the present.
- Appreciate that the technology of the future already exists but needs some improvements to change the world.
- Discuss the future of technologies for different industries.
- Identify the risks of the future of information technology.

14.2.- The speed of technological change

The beginning of the 20th century was an exciting time. Automobiles, telephones, radios, and airplanes became popular. The world could not remain the same. Mass production and scientific management brought advances to manufactured goods, making them cheaper and available to more people. Of course, it wasn't all wonderful. By the middle of that century, the world had gone through two world wars, but there were also the United Nations, color movies, live television, satellites, and transoceanic cables.

By the end of the 20th century, the computer was a commonly used tool; cell phones, music in MP3 format, and the Internet appeared. The world in the year 2000 was as different from that of 1950 as it was from 1900. The first decades of the 21st century were just as dizzying. Today, thinking about 1999 is like taking a trip to the distant past.

Forecasting what companies and the effect of technologies on society will be like in the mid to late 21st century is a job for tarot readers or fortune tellers with crystal balls. However, looking at what has happened in the past is enough to identify specific trends that can be extrapolated quite safely.

Forecasting the future requires analyzing what has changed and what has remained constant. It is sure that what has changed will continue to change and that the constants will remain.

14.3.- Today's world seen from the past

In 1958, two authors, Harold Leavitt and Thomas Whisler, published an article in the prestigious Harvard Business Review entitled "The Administration of the 1980s" [Leavitt & Whisler, 1958]. In a world where companies were growing increasingly complex, decentralizing and hiring more middle managers, they predicted that a new trend, which they called information technology, would allow senior managers to become more involved in the operation of their companies, recentralizing activities and reducing middle management. Information technology promised to allow fewer people to do more work; the lower the cost, the more companies would be willing to try it.

In an interview thirty years later, Leavitt indicates that they failed to predict the effect of miniaturization on desktop computers, making the decentralization of computing power feasible. Their vision's importance rests on focusing on the computer as a tool that could influence people's behavior and learning rather than on a machine to automate processes.

Lynda Applegate, James Cash, and Quinn Mills published in the same journal, but in 1988, an article analyzing the results of previous predictions and looking to the future [Applegate, Cash & Mills, 1988]. By focusing more on the effect of technologies, they predicted that many of the technological tools that would shape businesses already existed. They talked about knowledge-based systems, faster computers, better lines of communication, replacing the telephone with computers, and making speech into text easier. They analyzed the effect of these forecasts on the structure of organizations (making them more flexible and project-focused), administrative processes (storing the company's knowledge), and human resources (becoming more autonomous).

14.4.- What we can learn from past predictions

Many of the predictions made in the 1958 and 1988 articles have turned out to be correct. The first thing that is clear from the above forecasts is that the near future can be predicted if done carefully and responsibly. The second thing is that the technologies that will set the tone in the next 15 to 30 years already exist, and you can see their effects now. The third thing is that people will stay the same. We can concede that the person of the future may live longer or be healthier (the advances in biotechnology are impressive). Still, reasoning skills, response to innovations, and human reactions to political and social changes will stay the same or will change very slowly.

14.5.- The world of tomorrow as seen from today

The Technology Approach

It only takes a little intuition to know that technology, in the future, will be cheaper, more powerful, and more flexible. Information will be stored in large quantities and located using powerful search engines independent of the storage model. It's also not hard to see that the Internet, or the technology that replaces it, will influence civilization as much as the automobile did in the form of twentieth-century cities. We are already seeing the effect of working from home, which was required with the COVID-19 pandemic in 2020 and 2021. Can the Internet change the shape of businesses?

Product Focus

Before the Industrial Revolution, products were custom-made, one by one, in a slow and expensive process. The Industrial Revolution brought mass-produced items. The process was cheap, but the client had to adjust to what was available. The technological revolution allows us to manufacture products tailored to each customer but on a massive scale in a cheap process known as "mass customization." Making goods of good quality tailored to the customer and available to more people. Imagine if a company's services could be personalized, providing special attention to each customer.

The Business Solutions Approach

At the beginning of the 20th century, scientific management brought us improvements in control over work and support at the operational levels of the company. By the mid to late 20th century, information technology provided better control over information, supporting middle management.

At the end of the 20th century, knowledge management improved decisions, supporting top management. The first decades of the 21st century have brought power to the people. Social networks, crowdsourcing, cryptocurrencies, and mass customization have created societies with their own opinions and unprecedented control of coordination and autonomy.

Minicase – "The dress" a viral phenomenon

You're probably already familiar with the story. In February 2015. a lady (Cecilia Bleasdale) wanted to decide what dress to buy for her daughter's (Grace Johnston) wedding. She sends three photos to her daughter, saying she liked the third one better and asks for her opinion. The daughter told her that she agreed, that that white and gold dress would look good. The mother replied that there was no white and gold dress, it was blue and black. And the discussion began. They showed the photo to several friends and noticed that when they saw the same picture (at the same time), some saw it as white with gold, while others saw it as blue and black.

A friend (Caitlin McNeill) decided to upload the photo to Tumblr, a social network, and suddenly, it became a phenomenon. The whole planet discussed that dress and no one could agree on the color. [Wikipedia, 2020]

If you want to see the photograph, look for "the dress" or #thedress or #whiteandgold or #blackandblue. What color do you see that dress? Ask two other people.

180

Large companies will be able to get bigger without losing control. In contrast, through formal and informal networks, small companies will attack almost any market and project size by creating partnerships with specialists from other small companies worldwide, as needed for the projects. Do you see the potential to internationalize local companies?

Marketing Approach

Before the maturation of marketing, people found out about products through a word-of-mouth communication process, and advertising was tailored to each customer but had a minimal reach. With the emergence of the mass media, advertising began to be designed en masse, with a high reach but the same content for everyone.

Advances in Internet personalization technology, on-demand video and music services, and social media will tailor advertising to each user, providing high reach and low cost. The effects of these changes on advertising campaigns have already been felt.

Minicase – Personalized commercials on websites

Open a browser, enter a search engine like Google, search for information about a product (such as a sportswear brand, an electrical appliance, or a perfume), and then open Facebook or your email page. Check if the banners (commercials above or to the sides of your text) have anything to do with the product you searched for.

The Government's Approach

Like businesses, the government will have tailor-made products and services. The government will take advantage of the new opportunities provided by technology to offer services anytime, anywhere, and in any format, fulfilling its mission of better serving the people.

E-democracy will allow for greater citizen participation. Access to information will allow for better accountability and better allocation of responsibility to those in power, thus achieving a better use of resources.

14.6.- The risks of this vision

As in any story, the vision of the future does not come without imminent dangers. The first is security risk. With businesses becoming increasingly reliant on information and technology, data protection will be paramount in companies. The organization's knowledge and access to its equipment, systems, and data must be protected as tangible assets are now protected.

The second risk is vulnerability to critical failures, where a failure can destroy an organization (something like the Jurassic Park syndrome, the science fiction movie (the first in the series) where an attack on a computer sets the park's dinosaurs free, endangering its visitors). Securing against critical failures will require planning redundant systems and increasingly elaborate contingency plans, allowing a company to have complete backups of its systems and services in other cities or continents.

The third type of risk is that of losing privacy. The high availability of information will make creating a "big brother" very tempting, supervising people's every step. A social movement is expected to protect the rights of privacy and confidentiality needed to operate a free society, which in the long run has proven far more profitable than an oppressed society.

Minicase - Cyberattack Knocks Out of Gas on U.S. East Coast

In May 2021, gas stations on the East Coast of the United States, from Virginia to Florida to Alabama, were suddenly running out of fuel. The cause was that Colonial Pipeline, the company that managed a 5,500-mile pipeline, had to shut down operations because its computer systems were attacked by ransomware, and its computers could not operate. The company solved the problem quickly, but it would still take several days for the service to normalize. Even the president of the United States had to make a call to remain calm and not panic in the face of the temporary lack of fuel. [Greenberg, 2021; Caroll, Guerra, & Shah, 2021; Petras, et al., 2021]

14.7.- Conclusions

We've seen that things are still the same by looking at how things are different.

Technology may change, and problems may be different, but people, their needs, and satisfaction will remain the same.

The scale of human needs for food, shelter, and socialization will continue to apply to people. The view is, in general, optimistic. There will be better products, better information, and better quality of life. The risks are significant but surmountable. Forecasting what tomorrow's world will look like requires understanding today's world and the steps taken to get to where we are.

Our responsibility is to ensure that the world takes the shape we want through work and constant analysis of the changes that occur and their effects on society.

14.8.- Summary

- Predicting the direction technology will take in the future is possible.
- The future can be predicted by analyzing predictions of our present made in the past. The technologies that will change the world in the next 15 to 30 years already exist; their effects can be seen now, and people won't change much.
- The outlook for the future is, by and large, optimistic. There will be better products, better information, and better quality of life.
- There are security risks, vulnerability to critical flaws, and loss of privacy in this future vision, but they are surmountable.

14.9.- Review exercises

1. Identify a technology that exists in scientific labs but is only used by a few people. Find out why it has yet to hit the market (is it too expensive? Is it challenging to produce? Isn't it reliable?) and estimate how long it could take to solve those operational problems for the technology to become commonplace.

2. Find a photograph of the dress that the minicase of this chapter talks about and show the picture to three people. Did they all see the dress of the same color?
3. Interview an older person and ask them if they remember the world without cell phones. And how was the internet used at that time?
4. Look for an article discussing technology's future in a particular industry.

References

Chapter 1

[Alanís & García, 2020] Alanís, M., and García, P.R., "Tecnología de Información y la Práctica Contable: Una Visión Aplicada", ISBN: 9798621244439, Amazon, 2020.

[Babbage, 1864] Babbage, C. "Passages from the life of a philosopher" Longman, Roberts, & Green, London, (pp. 67), 1864.

[Davis & Olson, 1985] Davis, G.B., and Olson, M.H., "Management Information Systems: Conceptual Foundations, Structure and Development" second edition, McGraw-Hill, 1985.

[Senn, 1987] Senn, J.A. "Information Systems in Management" 3rd edition, Wadsworth Publishing, 1987.

[Sharda, Delen & Turban, 2015] Sharda, R., Delen, D., & Turban, E., "Business Intelligence, Analytics, and Data Science: A Managerial Perspective", ISBN: 978-0134633282, Pearson, 2017.

Chapter 2

[Anthony, 1965] Anthony, R. N. "Planning and Control Systems: a Framework for Analysis" Cambridge MA, Harvard University Press, 1965.

[DiCapua, et al., 2020] Di Capua, F., Tan, S., Wilkins, A., Thyagarajan, J., "Magic Quadrant for SAP S/4HANA Application Services, Worldwide" publication number G00407891, Gartner, April 2020.

[Faith, et al., 2020] Faith, T., Nguyen, D., Torii, D., Schenck, P., Hestermann, C., "Magic Quadrant for Cloud ERP for Product-Centric Enterprises," publication number G00377672, Gartner, June 2020.

[Gory & Scott-Morton, 1971] Gory G.A., and Scott-Morton, M.S. "A Framework for Management Information Systems", Sloan Management Review, Vol. 13, No. 1, Fall 1971.

[Hansen, et al., 2020] Hansen, I., Poulter, J., Elkin, N., Ferguson, C., "Magic Quadrant for CRM Lead Management" publication number G00463456, Gartner, August 2020.

[Laudon & Laudon, 2019] Laudon, K.C., and Laudon, J.P. "Management Information Systems: Managing the Digital Firm", 16th edition, Pearson Education, 2019.

[Manusama & LeBlanc, 2020] Manusama, B., LeBlanc, N., "Magic Quadrant for the CRM Customer Engagement Center" publication number G00432951, Gartner, June 2020.

[Salley, et al., 2021] Salley, A., Payne, T., Lund, P.O., "Magic Quadrant for Supply Chain Planning Solutions," document number G00450343, Gartner, February 2021.

[Sparks, et al., 2020] Sparks, B., Sullivan, P., van der Heiden, G., Longwood, J., "Magic Quadrant for CRM and Customer Experience Implementation Services", publication number G00386413, Gartner, April 2020.

[Turing, 1949] Turing, A. "The Mechanical Brain. Answer Found to 300-Year-Old Problem" The Times, London, pp. 4, col. 5, June 11, 1949.

Chapter 3

[BBC News World, 2019] BBC News Mundo, "Cambridge Analytica: the record fine that Facebook will have to pay for the way it handled the data of 87 million users" BBC News Mundo, July 24, 2019, accessed February 2024 in https://www.bbc.com/mundo/noticias-49093124

[Colosimo, 2015] Colosimo, K. "Bad Data is Scary! Here are 5 Stats to Prove It" Workato, October 31, 2015, accessed February 2024 in https://www.workato.com/blog/2015/10/bad-data-is-scary-here-are-5-stats-to-prove-it/#.WlGb7N_ibIU

[Davies & Rushe, 2019] Davies, R. & Rushe, D., "Facebook to pay $5bn fine as regulator settles Cambridge Analytica complaint" The Guardian, July

2019, accessed February 2024 in https://www.theguardian.com/technology/2019/jul/24/facebook-to-pay-5bn-fine-as-regulator-files-cambridge-analytica-complaint

[Doyle, 1891] Doyle, Arthur Conan, "A Scandal in Bohemia", London, 1891, reprinted Flowepot Press, United States, 2014.

[Gonzalez, 2020] Gonzalez, E. "Customer Experience: A Challenge for Retailers," Logistics Emphasis, April 14, 2020, accessed April 16, 2020, http://www.logisticamx.enfasis.com/notas/85631-customer-experience-reto-minoristas

[IDC, 2019] IDC, "Becoming a Best-Run Midsize Company: How Growing Companies Benefit from Intelligent Capabilities," IDC InfoBrief, sponsored by SAP, 2019.

[Jackson, 2024] Jackson, T. "Dashboards Vs. Scorecards: Deciding Between Operations & Strategy," Clearpoint Strategy, January 16, 2024, accessed February 2024 in, https://www.clearpointstrategy.com/dashboards-and-scorecards-deciding-between-operations-strategy/

[KR3dhead, 2018] KR3dhead "Full Microsoft R Open Predictive Analysis Software Review – What You Need to Know About Microsoft R Open", Skyose, August 12, 2018, accessed April 15, 2020 at https://skyose.com/full-microsoft-r-open-review/

[Kundu, 2016] Kundu, Anirban "Journey of Data: From Tables to Tiles – A sneak peek into the S/4 HANA Embedded Analytics Architecture". SAP Community, September 27, 2016, accessed February 2024, https://blogs.sap.com/2016/09/27/journey-of-datafrom-tables-to-tiles-a-sneak-peek-into-the-s4-hana-embedded-analytics-architecture/

[Meredith, 2918] Meredith, S., "Facebook-Cambridge Analytica: A timeline of the data hijacking scandal" CNBC, April 2018, accessed February 2024 on https://www.cnbc.com/2018/04/10/facebook-cambridge-analytica-a-timeline-of-the-data-hijacking-scandal.html

[Mora, et al., 2020] Mora Aristega, Julio Ernesto, et al., " El modelo COBIT 5 para auditoría y el control de los sistemas de información," Universidad Técnica de Babahoyo accessed February 2024 in https://repositorio.pucesa.edu.ec/bitstream/123456789/2355/1/Modelo%20Cobit.pdf

[Pat Research, 2021] Pat Research, "RapidMiner Studio," Pat Research, accessed February 2024 in https://www.predictiveanalyticstoday.com/rapidminer/

[Qualtrics, 2020] Qualtrics "Learn Customer Experience (CX) with Resources & Articles," Qualtrics, accessed April 16, 2020, https://www.qualtrics.com/experience-management/customer/

[Sisense, 2024] Sisense Team, "Scorecard vs Dashboard – What Each Adds to Business Intelligence", Sisense, accessed February 2024 in https://www.sisense.com/blog/scorecard-vs-dashboard-adds-business-intelligence/

Chapter 4

[Baca Urbina, 2007] Baca Urbina, G. "Fundamentos de Ingeniería Económica", 4ª edición, ISBN: 9789701061138, McGraw-Hill, 2007.

[Buffett, 1983] Buffett, W., "Chairman's Letter", March 3, 1983, consulted in January 2024 in https://www.berkshirehathaway.com/letters/1982.html

[Chandler, 1977] Chandler, A. D., "The Visible Hand. The Managerial Revolution in American Business", ISBN 0674940512, Harvard University Press, 1977.

[Laudon & Laudon, 2020] Laudon, K.C. & Laudon, J.P. "Management Information Systems: Managing the Digital Firm", 16th edition, ISBN: 978-0135191798, Pearson, 2020.

[Rifkin, 2014] Rifkin, J., "The Zero Marginal Cost Society: The Internet of things, the Collaborative Commons, and the Eclipse of Capitalism", ISBN 978-1-137-27846-3, Palgrave McMillan, 2014.

[Sullivan, Wicks & Luxhoj, 2004] Sullivan, W.G., Wicks, E.M., & Luxhoj, J.T., "Ingeniería Económica de DeGarmo", 12 edición, Pearson Educación, México, 2004.

Chapter 5

[Baca Urbina, 2015] Baca Urbina, G. "Ingeniería Económica" McGraw-Hill Interamericana, ISBN: 9786071512444, Mexico City, 2015.

[Franklin, 1748] Franklin, B., "Advice to a Young Tradesman Written by an Old One," Printed in George Fisher, The American Instructor: or Young Man's Best Companion. ... The Ninth Edition Revised and Corrected. Philadelphia: Printed by B. Franklin and D. Hall, at the New-Printing-Office, in Market-Street, 1748. pp. 375–7. Retrieved January 2024 from https://founders.archives.gov/documents/Franklin/01-03-02-0130

[Microsoft, 2024-1] Microsoft, "FV Function" accessed January 2024 in https://support.microsoft.com/en-us/office/fv-function-2eef9f44-a084-4c61-bdd8-4fe4bb1b71b3

[Microsoft, 2024-2] Microsoft, "PV Function" accessed January 2024 in https://support.microsoft.com/en-us/office/pv-function-23879d31-0e02-4321-be01-da16e8168cbd

[Microsoft, 2024-3] Microsoft, "NPV Function" accessed January 2024 in https://support.microsoft.com/en-us/office/npv-function-8672cb67-2576-4d07-b67b-ac28acf2a568

[Microsoft, 2024-4] Microsoft "IRR Function" accessed January 2024 in https://support.microsoft.com/en-us/office/irr-function-64925eaa-9988-495b-b290-3ad0c163c1bc

[Sullivan, Wicks & Luxhoj, 2004] Sullivan, W.G., Wicks, E.M., & Luxhoj, J.T., "DeGarmo Economic Engineering", 12th edition, Pearson Education, Mexico, 2004.

Chapter 6

[Alanís, 2020], Alanís, M., "La transformación Digital del Gobierno: Misma Tecnología, Diferentes Reglas, Mucho Más en Juego" Amazon, ISBN: 9798616079961, Middletown, DE, 2020.

[Cameron, 1963] Cameron, William Bruce, "Informal Sociology, a casual introduction to sociological thinking" Random House, New York. 1963.

[Cemex, 2021] Cemex, "Ley Sarbanes Oxley" consulted on January 2024 at https://www.cemex.com/es/inversionistas/gobierno-corporativo/ley-sarbanes-oxley#navigate

Chapter 7

[Brooks, 1972] Brooks, F.P. "The Mythical Man Month: Essays on Software Engineering"," Addison-Wesley Publishing Company, 1972.

[Chaudhari, 2016]   Chaudhari, K.;   "Importance of CMMI-DEV in COBITbased IT Governance" COBIT Focus; 4 January 2016, retrieved February 2024 from https://fdocuments.us/document/importance-of-cmmi-dev-in-cobit-based-it-governance.html

[Colorado, 2024] Colorado Division of Homeland Security & Emergency Management, "Continuity of Operations Plane] consulted January 2024 in https://dhsem.colorado.gov/emergency-management/plans/continuity-of-operations-plan

[Ford, 1922] Ford, H. in collaboration with Crowther, S., "My Life and Work" Doubleday, Page & Company, New York, 1922.

[Gefen and Zviran, 2006] Gefen, D.; Zviran, M.; "What can be Learned from CMMI Failures?" Communications of the Association for Information Systems, Vol. 17, 2006.

[Hammer, 1990] Hammer, Michael "Reengineering Work: Do not Automate, Obliterate" Harvard Business Review, Vol. 68, No. 4, 1990.

[Humphrey, 1988] Humphrey, W. S; "Characterizing the software process: a maturity framework" IEEE Software. 5 (2), March 1988.

[Kendall & Kendall, 2005] Kendall, K.E., and Kendall J.E. "Systems Analysis and Design" Sixth Edition, Pearson Education, 2005.

[Lankhorst et al., 2009] Lankhorst, M., et al.; "Enterprise Architecture at Work" The Enterprise Engineering Series, ISBN: 978-3-642-01309-6, Springer-Verlag Berlin Heidelberg 2009.

[Laudon and Laudon, 2020] Laudon, K.C. and Laudon, J.P. "Management Information Systems: Managing the Digital Firm" ISBN: 978-0135191798, Pearson, 2019.

Chapter 8

[Alanis, 2020] Alanis, M., "Tecnología de Información y la Práctica Contable", ISBN: 979861244439, 2020.

[Alanis, Kendall, & Kendall, 2009] Alanis, Macedonio; Kendall, Julie E.; Kendall, Kenneth E., "Reframing as Positive Design: An Exemplar from the Office of Civil Registry in Mexico" AMCIS 2009 Proceedings. Paper 268. San Francisco, CA: Association for Information Systems, 2009.

[Engwal, 2012] Engwal, M., "PERT, Polaris, and the realities of project execution", International Journal of Management Projects in Business, Vol 5, No. 4, pp 595-616, 2012, accessed February 2024 at https://www.researchgate.net/publication/263572044_PERT_Polaris_and_the_realities_of_project_execution

[Gantt.com, 2024] Gantt.com, "Gantt Chart History", Gantt.com accessed February 2024 at www.gantt.com

[Kendall & Kendall, 2005] Kendall, K.E., and Kendall J.E. "Systems Analysis and Design" Sixth Edition, Pearson Education, 2005.

[Laudon & Laudon, 2019] Laudon, K.C., and Laudon, J.P. "Management Information Systems: Managing the Digital Firm", 16th edition, Pearson Education, 2019.

[Sapolsky, 1972] Sapolsky, H.M., "The Polaris System Development" Harvard University Press, 1972, accessed February 2024 from http://ekt.bme.hu/CM-BSC-MSC/PERTReadings02.pdf

[Woods et al., 2019] Woods, W. D., Kemppanen, J., Turhanov, A., Waugh, L. "Day 3, part 2: 'Houston, we've had a problem'" Apollo Flight Journal, May 2017, accessed February 2024 at https://history.nasa.gov/afj/ap13fj/08day3-problem.html

Chapter 9

[Dickinson, 2018] Dickinson, D., "'Fake news' challenges audiences to tell fact from fiction" UN News, May 2018 Consulted January 2024 in https://news.un.org/en/audio/2018/05/1008682

[Friedman, 2005] Friedman, T.L., "It's a Flat World, After All," New York Times Magazine, April 3, 2005, pp. 32-37, New York, 2005.

[History, 2020] History.com Editors "Arab Spring" published January 2018, updated January 2020, consulted January 2023 in https://www.history.com/topics/middle-east/arab-spring

[Kahn & Dennis, 2022] Kahn, R., & Dennis M.A. "Internet Computer Network" Encyclopædia Britannica, Published June 2020, updated November 2022, consulted January 2023 in https://www.britannica.com/technology/Internet

[Laudon & Traver, 2018] Laudon, K. C., & Traver, C. G. "E-commerce: Business, Technology, Society" 14th Edition, ISBN: 9781292251707, Pearson, 2018.

[Poe, 1836] Poe, E.A., "Maelzel's Chess-Player" Southern Literary Messenger, April 1836.

[Porter, 2001] Porter M.E, "Strategy and the Internet" Harvard Business Review. March 2001, Vol. 79, Issue 3, pp. 62-78.

Chapter 10

[Alanis, 2020] Alanís, M. "La Transformación Digital del Gobierno: Misma Tecnología, Diferentes Reglas y Mucho Más en Juego" ISBN: 9798616079961, 2020.

[Cámara de Diputados del H. Congreso de la Unión, 2014] Cámara de Diputados del H. Congreso de la Unión "Ley de Adquisiciones, Arrendamientos y Servicios del Sector Público" New law published in the Diario Oficial de la Federación (Official Gazette of the Federation) on January 4, 2000, last reform published DOF 10-11-2014.

[Cámara de Diputados del H. Congreso de la Unión, 2019] Cámara de Diputados del H. Congreso de la Unión, "Constitución Política de los Estados Unidos Mexicanos" Last reform published DOF 09-08-2019.

[Government of Canada, 2024] Government of Canada, "The procurement process" consulted in January 2024 https://buyandsell.gc.ca/for-businesses/selling-to-the-government-of-canada/the-procurement-process

[Sun Tzu, Fifth Century BC] Sun Tzu. "The Art of War" originally published Fifth century BC. Consulted January 2024 in https://www.utoledo.edu/rotc/pdfs/the_art_of_war.pdf

Chapter 11

[Alanís, 2020] Alanís, M., "The Digital Transformation of Government: Same Technology, Different Rules, and Much More at Play", ISBN: 9798616079961, 2020.

[Dominguez 2009] Donminguez, J. "The Chaos Report 2009 on IT Project Failure", 2009, accessed January 2024 at https://pmhut.com/the-chaos-report-2009-on-it-project-failure

[Selig, 2008] Selig, Gad J., (2008) "Implementing IT Governance: A Practical Guide to Global Best Practices in IT Management", ISBN 978 90 8753119 5, Van Haren Publishing, 2008.

[Smith, 1776] Smith A. "The Wealth of Nations" book 1, chapter 1, original title: "An Inquiry into the Nature and Causes of the Wealth of Nations" London, 1776.

Chapter 12

[Bishop, 2006] Bishop, C.M. "Pattern Recognition and Machine Learning", Springer, 2006.

[Borbow, 1964] Borbow, D., "Natural Language Input for a Computer Problem Solving System", Ph.D. Dissertation, MIT, 1964.

[Cieslak, Mason & Vetter, 2019] Cieslak, D.; Mason, L.; Vetter,A. "What's 'critical' for CPAs to learn in an AI-powered world" Journal of Accountancy. Vol. 227 Issue 6, p1-6, June 2019.

[English, 2019] English, D.B.M., "The Rise of the (Accounting) Machines? Blockchain and AI: The Changing Face of the Profession" California CPA, Vol. 87 Issue 9, p12-14, May 2019.

[Gartner, 2021] Gartner, "About Us," Gartner Inc., accessed June 2021 in https://www.gartner.com/en/about

[Keenoy, 1958] Keenoy, C.L. "The impact of automation on the field of accounting," The Accounting Review 33(2): 230–236, 1958.

[Kokina & Davenport, 2017] Kokina, J. & Davenport, T.H., "The Emergence of Artificial Intelligence: How Automation is Changing Auditing", Journal of Emerging Technologies in Accounting, Vol. 14 Issue 1, p115-122, 2017.

[Macari and Krensky, 2023] Macari E. and Krensky, P., "Hype Cycle for Analytics and Business Intelligence, 2023", Document Number G00792723, Gartner Inc., July 27, 2023.

[Mitchel, 1996] Mitchell, M. "An Introduction to Genetic Algorithms" MIT Press. Cambridge, MA, 1996.

[Nakamoto, 2008], Nakamoto, S. "Bitcoin: A peer-to-peer electronic cash system" bitcoin.org, reviewed March 2020 in www.bitcoin.org/bitcoin.pdf

[Nietzsche, 1873] Nietzsche, F. "Philosophy in the Tragic Age of the Greeks", Regnery Publishing Inc. ISBN 0-89526-944-9, posthumous publication 1962, reprinted 1998.

[Schank, 1972] Schank, R.C. "Conceptual Dependancy: A Theory of Natural Language Understanding," Cognitive Psychology, 3, 552-631, 1972.

[ScienceSoft, 2024] ScienceSoft, "Data Analytics Services", ScienceSoft, accessed February 2024 in https://www.scnsoft.com/services/analytics

[Simon, 1981], Simon, H.A., "The Sciences of the Artificial" Second Edition, MIT Press, Cambridge, MA, 1981.

[Yahoo, 2024] Yahoo Finance, "cryptocurrencies", accessed February 2024 in https://finance.yahoo.com/crypto/

Chapter 13

[Alanis, 1991] Alanis, M., "Controlling the Introduction of Strategic Information Technologies" in "Management Impacts of Information Technology: Perspectives on Organizational Change and Growth" E. Szewczak, C. Snodgrass, and M. Khosrowpour, editors, Idea Group Publishing, Harrisburg, PA, 1991.

[Alanís, 2010] Alanís, M., "Manejo de la Introducción de la Innovación Tecnológica en la Educación", in "Tecnología Educativa y Redes de Aprendizaje de Colaboración: Retos y Realidades de Innovación en el Ambiente Educativo", Burgos Aguilar, J.V. & Lozano Rodríguez, A., Editors, Mexico, Editorial Limusa, March 2010.

[Brancheau, 1987] Brancheau, J.C., "The Diffusion of Information Technology: Testing and Extending Innovation Diffusion Theory in the

Context of End-User Computing", Doctoral Dissertation, University of Minnesota, Minneapolis, MN, 1987.

[Gallagher, 2023] Gallagher, W., "Newton launched August 2, 1993 setting the stage for what would become the iPad and iPhone", Apple insider, August 2023. Retrieved February 2024 from https://appleinsider.com/articles/18/08/02/newton-launched-august-2-1993-setting-the-stage-for-what-would-become-the-ipad-and-iphone

[Gilbert & Varanasi, 2023] Gilbert, B., & Varanasi, L., "33 of the biggest failed products from the world's biggest companies," Insider, August 2023, retrieved February 2024 from https://www.businessinsider.com/biggest-product-flops-in-history-2016-12?r=MX&IR=T

[Hein, 2018] Hein, B., "Massive lines form at Apple stores for iPhone XS launch", Cult of Mac, September 2018. Retrieved February 2024 from https://www.cultofmac.com/577959/massive-lines-forming-at-apple-stores-in-anticipation-of-iphone-xs-launch/

[Machiavelli, 1532] Machiavelli, N. "The Prince" (Chapter VI), 1532, translation published by Penguin Random House, UK, 2009, consulted February 2024 in https://apeiron.iulm.it/retrieve/handle/10808/4129/46589/Machiavelli%2C%20The%20Prince.pdf

[Rogers, 2003] Rogers, E. M. "Diffusion of Innovations" (5th ed.). New York: Free Press, 2003.

[Wuerthele, 2017] Wuerthele, M., "Giant lines forming at Apple stores internationally in advance of iPhone X sales" Apple insider, Nov 02, 2017. Retrieved February 2024 from https://appleinsider.com/articles/17/11/02/giant-lines-forming-at-apple-stores-internationally-in-advance-of-iphone-x-sales

Chapter 14

[Applegate, Cash, & Mills, 1988] Applegate, L. M., J. I. Cash, and Q. D. Mills. "Information Technology and Tomorrow's Manager." Harvard Business Review, Vol. 66, No. 6, 1988.

[Caroll, War, & Shah, 2021] Carroll, J., Guerra Luz.,A., Shah,J.R., "Gas Stations Run Dry as Pipeline Races to Recover From Hacking" Bloomberg, 5-8-2021, accessed May 2021 in https://www.bloomberg.com/news/articles/2021-05-09/u-s-fuel-sellers-scramble-for-alternatives-to-hacked-pipeline

[Dickens, 1843] Dickens, C., "A Christmas Carol" Chapman & Hall, London, 1843. Retrieved February 2024 from https://www.ibiblio.org/ebooks/Dickens/Carol/Dickens_Carol.pdf

[Greenberg, 2021] Greenberg, A., "The Colonial Pipeline Hack Is a New Extreme for Ransomware," Wired, 5-8-2021, accessed May 2021 at https://www.wired.com/story/colonial-pipeline-ransomware-attack/

[Leavitt & Whisler, 1958] Leavitt, H. and T. Whisler, "Management in the 1980's," Harvard Business Review, Vol. 36 No. 6, 1958.

[Petras, et al., 2021] Petras, G., Loehrke, J., Beard, S.J., Padilla, R., "US gas prices rise as Colonial Pipeline reopens after ransomware attack", USA Today, May 10, 2021, accessed May 2021 in https://www.usatoday.com/in-depth/graphics/2021/05/10/colonial-pipeline-closed-hackers-ransomware-gasoline-jet-fuel-cybercrime/5019625001/

[Wikipedia, 2020] Wikipedia, "The Dress" Wikipedia, 2020, accessed April 2020 from https://en.wikipedia.org/wiki/The_dress

About the Author
Dr. Macedonio Alanís

alanis@tec.mx   maalanis@hotmail.com

Dr. Macedonio Alanis is Full Professor of Management Information Systems at Tecnologico de Monterrey (ITESM), in Monterrey, Mexico. He has published eight books and more than 120 papers, book chapters, and conferences on topics such as Digital Transformation, Business Intelligence, Strategic IT Management, and Educational Technology. He also designed and worked on a joint IT management program with Carnegie Mellon University and a joint specialization program in project management with Stanford University. Some of his classes, using distance learning, are attended live by nearly 1000 students in nine Latin American countries.

In the private sector, Dr. Alanis has been the CFO of Neoris, an IT company of the multinational CEMEX (NYSE: CX). He created Global Software Factory, a co-investment between CEMEX and World Software Services, developing IT projects in Mexico, Europe, the US, and South America. He has worked as a solutions architect for IBM and is part of Cutter Consortium's group of expert consultants.

In the public sector, he worked as CIO for the Government of the State of Nuevo Leon. He was elected president of CIAPEM, the National Association of States and Cities Chief Information Officers in Mexico. He also participated in the definition of Mexico's national IT policies.

Dr. Alanis received the prestigious Eisenhower Fellowship and was elected to occupy the Americas Chair on the Association for Information Systems (AIS) Board of Directors.

Dr. Alanis holds a Ph.D. in Business Administration with a concentration on Management Information Systems from the University of Minnesota. He obtained a Master of Sciences in Computer Science (ScM) from Brown University and a BSc in Computer Science from Tecnologico de Monterrey in Monterrey, Mexico.